GREENW

3 8028 0

D1580051

Bᴏ

The
Able
Seaman

Illustrations by M. Halyard

THE
ABLE
SEAMAN

A Basic Book of Boating Under Sail or Power

by EVERETT B. MORRIS

HARPER & BROTHERS, PUBLISHERS · NEW YORK

THE ABLE SEAMAN

The courtesy of the Evinrude Boating Foundation in permitting the use here of some of the
material written by the author for "Outboard
Boating Skills" is gratefully acknowledged by
him and the publisher.

Library of Congress catalog card number: 60-7547

To all of those patient, forebearing seamen
who guided me through my apprenticeship afloat

Contents

Preface

NEPTUNE'S realm is a world far removed from the treadmill of daily dullness, of care and pressing responsibility. His watery kingdom is peopled by those who enjoy fun and warm companionship, who appreciate the boon of peace, who can balance relaxation with moments of high excitement, and know the glow of satisfaction that is the reward of a seamanlike job.

For steadily increasing and impressive numbers of people Neptune's trident is the symbol of a new-found freedom, an escape from workaday worries into a world where every skipper is his own king. Today, boating in all of its forms is one of our country's most popular and populous participation sports.

For those who are taking their first hesitant steps toward laying out a course to pleasure afloat, this book is intended as a steadying, helping hand. It does not pretend to be an encyclopedia of sea-going knowledge. Neither will it make an able seaman out of a landlubber overnight. That is not its aim. Rather it is my objective to provide boating's recent recruit with enough fundamental knowledge and guidance to enable him to enjoy his sport with the maximum of pleasure and safety and a minimum of difficulties. A veteran skipper may enjoy guiding a less experienced sailor with the help of this book. For it is my hope that familiarity with the following pages will aid the reader to build a solid foundation for the skills that will develop as his experience in and around boats grows.

The able seaman, no matter where his preference lies with

respect to type of craft, or whether he exercises his skills on lake, river, ocean, slough or bayou, is always a welcome hand on any boat.

E. B. M.

February 1, 1960

The
Able
Seaman

CHAPTER 1

Boats and Motors and Sails

DINGHIES, prams; catboats and canoes; sloops, scows and skiffs; runabouts and knockabouts; cutters and catamarans; motor yachts, cruisers, ketches, motor sailers, schooners, yawls and houseboats. Racing craft and family boats. Big boats, little boats; slim boats, fat boats. Boats that bear too close a resemblance to chrome-trimmed, two-toned, porcelain bathtubs; boats that look like space rockets; boats that look like boats.

Wind-driven boats; others that rely on engines for propulsion —engines installed in the boat, engines hung over the stern; engines which burn gasoline, engines whose tipple is diesel oil.

There are wooden boats, and those fashioned of blends of fiberglass and resin, and other modern products of the chemical laboratory; boats stamped out of aluminum, fabricated of steel, sheet plywood, canvas and rubber.

Their bottoms are flat, round, vee or inverted vee in shape. Some plow through the water, others skim over it. There are hydroplanes and hydrofoils. Some hulls are pierced for centerboards; some are fitted with outside lead or iron ballast keels; others are fitted with boards in both bilges.

There are boats built to meet the special needs of a special owner; boats that reflects the individuality of their designers or the whimsies of backyard builders; boats punched out on production lines, that come out as alike as shocks in a wheat field.

These are the ships of our huge, still growing pleasure fleet, a

1

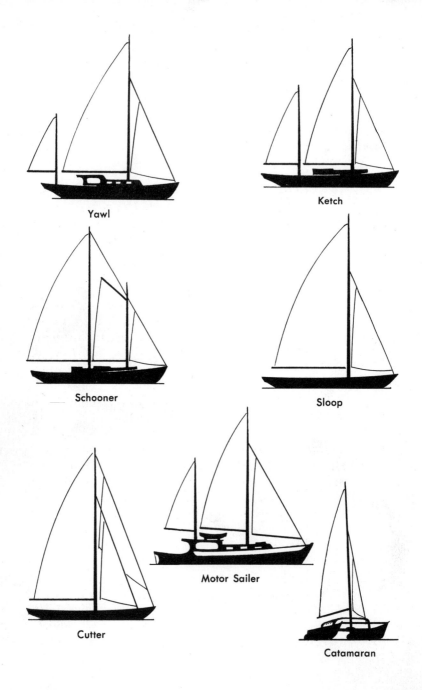

Yawl

Ketch

Schooner

Sloop

Cutter

Motor Sailer

Catamaran

vast navy whose units are based wherever there is water enough to float them—and nature has bordered, etched and splashed our map with the blue that denotes rivers, lakes and seas.

Small wonder then that the incipient boatman hesitates on the doorstep to his new sport, uncertain, confused, bewildered. Which boat to select as the medium for launching himself into the sport? Isn't selection too complicated for the uninitiated?

MAKING A CHOICE

Really, there is nothing occult or even difficult about sorting the boats. Once you understand even a little about what different boats can do and what they cannot do, and once you have the answers to these three simple questions, the rest is easy:

Do you prefer motor or sail?

For what use is the boat intended?

Where will it be used—in what waters?

Glib salesmen often tell starry-eyed prospects that "handling a motorboat is just like driving an automobile." That statement is intended to give the impression that the veriest landlubber can become a master mariner overnight. Nothing could be further from the truth. Boat handling just isn't that simple. Learning to get from place to place in a motorboat, be it inboard or outboard powered, is easier than learning how to sail, but it still requires application, intelligence and an understanding of the boat's capabilities and limitations.

Those who take the salesman at his word, leap into a boat, start the engine, open the throttle wide and speed through a crowded anchorage are those who keep the repair yards busy and inspire lawmakers to write legislation restricting the activities of good boating people as well as the menaces.

If your taste runs to speed, if it is necessary for you to get from here to there with reasonable dispatch, if you enjoy tinkering with motors and things mechanical, then a motor boat is your dish. If you like the challenge of marrying wind and sail, if you're one to appreciate the thrill of making an inanimate thing of wood and cloth and wire come to life when a breeze ripples the water, then engines are for the other fellow, not you.

The next step is to consider what you intend to do with the

boat and where you plan to do it. The type of craft ideal for fishing on a slow-flowing, shallow river, or sheltered pond, would be the wrong boat entirely for negotiating coastal waterways where tidal currents, strong breezes and the wakes of passing vessels make the going bumpy.

By the same token, a sturdy, high-powered 35-foot offshore sport fishing cruiser would be completely out of place in waters abounding in snags and sandbars, and so confined that the yacht could not go anywhere without meeting itself coming back.

And if it's competition that you seek, if the race course beckons, you will be needing something quick and lively and responsive. No fat, deep, sluggish family day boat for you.

There are all sorts of examples of the wrong boat for the wrong job, inefficient combinations of motor and hull, poorly conceived and carelessly rigged sailboats, under-powered boats, over-powered boats and boats that are innately cranky and perverse. You can avoid mistakes, though, by the exercise of plain, everyday common sense (something which seems to melt away when a lad or a lass gets starry-eyed over a boat), by heeding the instructions of reputable boat builders and manufacturers of engines, and by taking the time to learn just a few things about different kinds of boats, principally what they can do and what they cannot do.

BASIC DESIGNS AND ABILITIES

To begin the lesson, let's take a look at the good, old-fashioned, flat-bottomed rowboat—or skiff, as it is sometimes called. With

Skiff   Pram

its straight, slightly flared sides and a bottom almost as level as a dance floor, the skiff is easy to build and relatively inexpensive whether it be constructed of sawn planks and ribs, plywood or aluminum. With an outboard motor of 5 horsepower or less, the flat-bottomed skiff makes a satisfactory fishing or utility craft for shallow or protected waters. Fitted with a centerboard and the simplest of sailing rigs, it will get around when the breeze blows. It won't thrill you with its speed and handling qualities under power or sail. It isn't meant to. It is a plain, honest working boat that will do well the job for which it was intended. Glamor is no part of its make-up.

A pram is a rowboat with its nose bobbed; that is, squared off. It has more room and stability forward and, because of its peculiar bow shape, will tow better than a skiff. For that reason, and because of their generally small size (7 to 10 feet), prams are popular as tenders for auxiliary cruising yachts and inboard cabin cruisers. They are adaptable for use with small outboard engines, and many are built with centerboards or dagger boards and a demountable rig so that they can be sailed.

As a matter of fact there are whole fleets of sailing prams in some parts of the country—notably Florida and California—where they are used to give boys and girls their first taste of competition under sail.

Many persons tend to dislike round-bottomed boats because they are "tippy." Boats don't tip; people tip boats. There is no reason why a well designed, properly built round-bottom boat of ample beam—plenty of width, that is, in relation to length—should not be a good, stable rough-water craft. Boats of this form are normally more easily driven and maneuvered than flat-bottomed skiffs. Most of the outboard runabouts, from 12 to 18 feet in length, particularly in this age of molded plywood and molded fiberglass construction, are round bottomed. Dinghies, by the way, are merely small round-bottomed boats for use with oars, the smallest outboards, sail, or all three at different times. Like prams, they are used as tenders for larger vessels and for teaching the fundamentals of sailing to the young.

The vee-bottomed boat is a popular outboard hull form, especially when the emphasis is on speed. It is a much better rough-water boat than the flat bottom, but it has to be strongly built to withstand the pounding it takes. Moderate vee sections are found in many of the one-design classes of small racing sailboats. It is easier, quicker and therefore cheaper to build vee-type hulls than those with curves and rounded sections.

Now to explain the difference between "displacement" hulls and "planing" hulls. It is quite simple: displacement boats are designed to run *through* the water; planing boat is designed to run *on* or *over* the water.

Planing Hull   Displacement Hull

Most outboard boats are designed to plane—skip along the surface—when they attain a certain speed. Some though, being of the heavy displacement type, will go only so fast no matter how much power is applied. If you hang too large a motor on the transom, all that will happen is that the stern will squat and drag up a nice big wave to follow the boat. What you are doing, then, is wasting gasoline, making a big fuss in the water and going nowhere that you couldn't get to better with less power and bother.

This is a good time to learn that because a certain boat will run at 15 miles an hour with a 15-horsepower motor, it won't go 30 miles an hour if you increase the power to 30. The reason lies in what naval architecture calls speed-length ratio, and in the peculiarities of hull design. Too much power is wasteful—and dangerous.

You can over-power sailboats, too, by carrying too much sail when the wind velocity increases. That is why reef points are fitted to mainsails and why there are different sized jibs for the same boat.

A boat with a broad, flat bottom aft of amidships, provided that construction weights are distributed properly in the hull and the vessel is not overloaded, will tend to climb out of the water as its speed increases. This is as true of some types of sailing craft as it is of motorboats. At top speed, the boat will level off and skim along on top of the water with only a small portion of the bottom and the outboard motor's lower unit in the water. A sailboat "on the plane" will appear to be riding on an air cushion. The vee bottom lends itself readily to planing.

Another type of planing hull is the hydroplane or "step" boat normally used only for racing under power. The hydroplane has a step-like break across the bottom of the boat from one side to the other, usually a little aft of amidships. This notch creates an air cushion behind the step when the boat is moving forward, reduces the amount of bottom surface exposed to water friction and lifts the boat into planing position on top of the water. When a hydroplane is running properly, it is said to be "riding on its step." Boats with more than one step are called multi-step hydroplanes, and others, with a series of shallow steps along the bottom, have "shingled" bottoms.

CONSTRUCTION

In the current era of production line boat building we encounter many different types of small boat construction. Only a few years ago, the twentieth century version of the Indian birch bark canoe was a frail craft fashioned of canvas stretched over very light, thin wooden ribs. Today you frequently find it stamped out of one sheet of aluminum—a stronger, leak-proof canoe and one much less likely to come to grief on rocks and sunken stumps.

Dinghies used to be put together of frames and planks, and sometimes made in the same way as canoes if lightness was the prime requisite. Rowboats, either round or flat bottomed, were likewise frame and plank construction. So, of course, were the larger boats: cruisers, runabouts, racing and cruising sailing yachts.

It is all changed now. The trend is toward lighter, easier-to-mass-produce boats that can—in the case of the small to medium-sized units—be moved around the country like so much baggage. The smaller boats can be carried from home to lake to river to harbor on top of the family car, in much the same way that skiers transport their equipment. Boats too large or bulky for this method of moving can be hauled behind an automobile either on trailers designed especially for such tasks, or in the case of a few ingeniously fitted amphibious craft, on their own wheels.

Besides being lighter and easier to move about, the modern

one-piece hulls molded or shaped from synthetics, plywood and aluminum alloys are easier to maintain. They are less suscepti-ble to damage, too; hence their steadily growing sales.

Some are good in some waters, some are good in others, some are likely to serve and perform well almost anywhere. The choice comes down to personal preference and, quite often, to pocket-book.

Lapstrake Construction

Smooth-planked Construction

Basically, there are two kinds of wooden hull construction: smooth-planked or carvel-built, and lapstrake or clinker-built. The latter form, incidentally, has been imitated successfully in molded fiberglass reinforced resin.

Lapstrake, characteristic of the famed Jersey sea skiff and a style used by many builders of rugged, heavy duty runabouts and cruisers, gets its name from the method of putting the planking, or shell, of the boat together. The bottom edge of each plank over-laps the edge of the one below. The planks are fastened together along these laps with copper rivets, bolts or clinch nails, and the ribs, or frames, to which they are later attached, are fitted into the hull after all of the planking is done. Great strength for relatively light weight of materials is claimed for this con-struction.

Smooth-planked hulls have their frames set up first and then the planks, set edge to edge, are nailed, screwed or riveted to the ribs. A variation on this basic theme is called strip planking. In this case, the planks are cut into narrow strips, set edge to edge and then nailed together from top to bottom—edge nailing, it is called. Fewer ribs and transverse strength members are required in this method which produces a smooth, strong shell. Strip planking has been used with success in combination with fiberglass sheathing for the outside of the hull. The result is a hard, shiny finish and a dry interior.

Another form of smooth hull is achieved by building up layers of plywood and tough marine glue over a form and then molding it under heat and high pressure into a one-piece shell that cannot leak because it has no seams, and is so strong inherently that it requires very few frames, if any. In larger boats built in this fashion, the normal below-decks bulkheads act as transverse supports.

Other smooth hulls are built of sheet plywood, one-piece aluminum or welded aluminum plates, and, of course, various synthetics. In metal and fiberglass boats it is the practice to make air chambers and flotation tanks integral to the hulls. Wooden boats, of course, provide their own buoyancy when swamped or capsized, but this factor has to be built into boats made of materials that will not float naturally.

POWER

There is a boat for every purpose and a purpose for every boat. If what you seek does not exist, you will have no difficulty finding a naval architect who will design it for you. There is the right motor for the right boat, too, and getting them together to form an efficient, economical, reliable team is much easier than you might think. In their catalogs and handbooks, outboard manufacturers are very definite about which engine to use with what boat. In the case of boats with inboard engines you usually have to assume that the builder neither under-powered nor over-powered his product. The question of a power plant, i.e., sail plan, for one-design racing craft or stock day sailers and cruising vessels, has been answered by the designer, or by class restrictions.

In the case of outboard boats, the builders make it a point to recommend engines of a certain horsepower for use with boats of a certain length and beam. It makes good sense to follow these recommendations. No one knows better than the builder just what it takes to make one of his boats perform her best.

In this connection, another good guide is the Outboard Boating Club of America, which has its headquarters in Chicago. This organization, supported by outboard engine, boat, and trailer manufacturers, specializes in service for the outboard owner. It conducts field tests and, as a result of them, makes up a table of boat and engine capabilities. Every boat built to OBC approved specifications carries on its transom a metal plate which tells the maximum number of pounds the hull was built to carry and the largest size motor with which it can be used under normal conditions.

PICKING A SAILBOAT

Newcomers to sailing have different problems than those of their mechanically inclined brethren of the water. If all they are seeking is a comfortable, roomy, moderately rigged boat for day sailing and leisurely knocking about, they face few worries. It will be mostly a matter of selecting the boat that pleases the eye, meets space requirements, suits the waters in which it is to be used, and fits the pocketbook. Whether it is to be a keel or centerboard boat depends to some extent on whether the home waters are shallow or deep, and again, in some cases, on the size of the purchaser's bankroll. Keel boats, with their expensive lead or cast iron outside ballast, cost more in some types.

If the beginner has his eye on a racing career, then he had best be guided by what class or classes are raced where he intends to do his sailing. There is no point in buying a Comet Class sloop if all of the other racing boats on the lake are Rebels, Lightnings, Thistles or something else. The Comet would have nothing to race against.

Virtually all of the small boat racing on this continent is done in one-design or severely restricted classes. Nothing is quite so lonesome, quite so valueless as an orphan racing sailboat. There is another thing to remember about buying into an established class: you always have a market for your boat when you decide to go into something larger, or to take up cruising.

A word on buying a second hand, or any used boat. There are no cheap good boats, and real bargains are as rare as orchids in Antarctica.

If you are going to buy a used boat, be sure to take along someone who truly knows what it is all about—someone who knows that paint can hide many frailties, knows where to look for dry rot, broken frames, cracked planking, corroded rigging and so on. If you haven't a friend competent to help in the inspection of a used boat, then by all means retain the services of a professional surveyor. He'll be worth every cent he charges. His fee will depend largely on the size of the boat to be surveyed.

There are incipient boatmen who don't quite have the price of a boat ready to sail or drive away. This doesn't mean that they must remain ashore. If they have any facility with ordinary tools, paint brush and putty knife, they can build their own boats from low-cost prefabricated kits. These are marketed in various forms.

For molded plywood or fiberglass boats, you can buy the bare hull and then finish it with either your own materials or the essential parts supplied by the builder. This, of course, is somewhat more expensive than starting from scratch and assembling the pre-cut stem, keel, frames, planking, transom and deck that come with assembly instructions, glue, seam compound and fastenings.

How well this sort of operation turns out depends upon how carefully you follow instructions and how much time you put into sandpapering and finishing. A word of advice at this point. Unless you are fortunate enough to be able to count on experienced assistance, don't tackle too large and complicated a job. Try something reasonably small and simple the first time.

CHAPTER 2

Equipment and Safety

PROPER equipment for the boat and safety afloat are inter-related. Having the right equipment on board won't necessarily make your craft safe or you a safe boatman, but you cannot have a safe boat without proper equipment.

Just what is the right equipment gets back to the question of boat size, use and location. It should be obvious that what is more than adequate for a 12-foot sailboat would not begin to do the job for a 20-foot inboard runabout or small outboard cruiser.

The Coast Guard lays down the rules for boats operating on waters under its jurisdiction. States have, or are about to have, laws governing equipment on boats based on rivers, ponds and lakes wholly within their cognizance. There are some variations, of course, but by and large the Coast Guard sets the pattern.

The Coast Guard enforces different federal rules for different sizes of motorboats—and this includes sailing craft with auxiliary motors. Generally speaking, outboard boats must meet the same requirements for safety equipment as specified for the general classes of motorboats of identical length. Exceptions are made, however, with respect to engine ventilation, carburetor flame arrestors and the carrying of fire extinguishers.

You can find out the requirements for your particular boat by applying to the Coast Guard for its *Pleasure Craft* folder (CG-290), consulting the local flotilla of the Coast Guard Auxiliary or unit of the United States Power Squadron, or applying to the appropriate department in your state.

The rule of common sense, of good boating practice, takes precedence over legal rules where maximum safety is concerned. It pays to err on the side of extra equipment rather than to get by on the bare requirement. Let us take, for example, a 14-foot utility outboard runabout and fit it out properly—that is, with all of the safety equipment required by law and the gear that will make her "well found."

ESSENTIAL FOR SAFETY

First a Coast Guard approved life preserver, buoyant vest, ring buoy, or buoyant cushion for every person on board. This requirement can be met in whole or in part by using cushions that are nice to sit on and efficient in emergencies. They can be made of kapok, fibrous glass, or plastic foam covered with canvas or plastic fabric, and fitted with grab straps.

These straps can be slipped over the shoulders so that the cushion becomes a life preserver worn on the chest or the back. Perhaps the best way to wear one in an emergency is with one arm slipped through one strap and the opposite leg through the other. They stay on better that way.

If there is anyone in the boat who cannot swim, he should wear a life vest at all times. There are many good jackets or vests on the market now that are neither bulky nor clumsy, They fit well, come in attractive colors, and, what is more important, provide positive flotation in the water.

The law does not require open outboards of less than 16 feet overall length to carry a fire extinguisher, but wherever there is gasoline it is a good idea to have a chemical fire dousing implement around. Besides, you never know when you may need it to help someone else.

Don't leave the extinguisher rolling around in the bottom of the boat, or hidden under the foredeck amid the clutter of anchor rode, oil cans and what-not. A mounting bracket comes with an extinguisher when you buy it; attach this to a frame, bulkhead or seat handy to the steering position where you can get your hands on the extinguisher quickly when it is needed.

Get an anchor—one of the lightweight, folding type will do— and 100 feet of ⅜-inch nylon line, or ½-inch manila line for it.

You never know when you are going to need an anchor that will hold, and a long, strong length of rope to keep you where you are while you refill the fuel tank or make an engine repair. And it is just what the doctor ordered to keep you from drifting onto a rocky lee shore when a hard squall strikes and the motor packs

Light-weight folding anchor

up. Two 20-foot lengths of the same material as your anchor line will do nicely as dock lines, one for the bow and the other for the stern.

BASIC EQUIPMENT LIST

Here is a list of items that you should keep on board, preferably in a locker or drawer built under a seat and thus in no one's way:

Flashlight (learn how to signal with it)

Flares or smoke signals (for distress and breakdown situations)

Whistle (motorboats) or foghorn (sailboats)

Box compass (if you're going cruising or into open water)

Three fenders (there are some excellent light rubber and plastic foam fenders on the market) to protect rail and topsides when lying alongside a pier, or tied up to another boat

First aid kit (you never know when you are going to need it)

Paddle (even the modern engine quits once in a while, the gas tank runs dry, or you forget to bring a spare shearpin)

Tool kit (pliers, screw driver, patented wrench, cotter pins, extra spark plugs, shearpins, spare propeller and nut)

Besides these, you should carry a reserve fuel supply, a container of drinking water or, if you're boating on a pure lake, something with which to scoop up a serving; a bailing can, sponge and canvas ditty bag for odds and ends.

Evinrude Boating Foundation

Fenders protect the hull of this boat lying alongside a float.

A heavy canvas tote bag is a most useful boat accessory. You can use it to carry ice, or numerous packages, aboard. When it is empty, it folds away into a very small space, or—still folded—it can be used as a cushion on an unupholstered seat.

EXTRA ITEMS FOR THE SAILBOAT

If you are sailing a 14- to 20-foot boat instead of skipping around in a 14-foot outboard runabout, there are a few adjustments you will have to make in the equipment list. Life preservers, anchor and plenty of rode are, of course, just as essential to a sailboat as they are to a boat that depends on gasoline for motive power.

You will still need flashlight, flares, horn, compass, fenders and first aid kit. When the wind leaves you flat, a paddle is wonderful to have at hand. The tool kit will differ somewhat: you'll still need pliers, screw driver, patented wrench and cotter pins, but you should carry a few spare shackles and sail slides. The ditty bag is a very good idea, too, for sail stops, odd bits of line, palm, needle and sail twine, and a knife with marlinspike.

You'll need the bailing can, sponge and fresh water container, and you'll also need a good stiff brush and some bits of hard canvas for rubbing down the bottom before the day's race.

IF YOU CAPSIZE

This is as good a place as any to lay down the safe procedure to follow when a capsize occurs, for we must recognize the fact that accidents do happen and be prepared properly to handle them. Centerboard sailboats are susceptible to capsizes resulting from careless or reckless handling. Motorboats can roll over or swamp when overloaded, badly handled, or driven by hare-brained exhibitionists.

We're less concerned here with the causes of capsizes than with what to do when they occur, but it will be helpful to brief some of the unseamanlike actions that precipitate impromptu swimming parties, sometimes with serious consequences.

In a breeze strong enough to keep the crew on the rail of a sailboat to reduce the angle of heel, the most common causes of capsizes are (1) having a sheet belayed (made fast to its cleat) instead of being held in the hand so that it can be eased quickly; (2) trying to see just how far the boat can be heeled ("tipped") in a hard puff without going over; and (3) attempting to lug sail through the wind shifts and flukes of a squall instead of getting sail off.

Small motor driven craft get into trouble when they have too many persons on board, fail to angle across the heavy wakes of larger boats, turn too sharply in rough water, or try to plow through a bad squall with wind and sea on the beam instead of running slowly head to it, or anchoring.

When a capsize or swamping happens there are two cardinal rules to follow. (1) Don't panic; and (2) stay with the boat.

The next thing to do, assuming that you are not already wearing one, is to get into a life preserve, or slip your arms through the loops of a buoyant cushion. This applies even though you may be a strong swimmer. Even good swimmers get tired, and immersion in cold water quickly reduces staying power.

Next, count heads; make certain that all hands are accounted for and in good shape. It is always possible that someone has been stunned by the boom, become entangled in rigging, or struck his head on the rail. Render the necessary assistance.

Aetna Casualty & Surety Company

Passengers sit on opposite gunwale to balance the boat and prevent capsizing while the one being rescued is helped aboard. She has been using a cushion as a life preserver.

Let's assume that everyone is all right, wearing a lifejacket, and either sitting on the overturned boat or holding onto it. You will note another assumption—that the boat floats. We so assume because you should *never* go out in a small boat that is unable to support its crew in the water even when it is filled.

Wooden hulls—those without heavy lead or cast iron keels— have enough natural buoyancy to keep them up. Metal and fiberglass boats have to be built with watertight compartments or tanks, or fitted with blocks of styrofoam or similar buoyant substance, to prevent them from sinking.

If the capsize occurs in the course of a race, or on a busy waterway, help will be on its way to you in minutes. If it happens in a lonely spot where no one is likely to notice your plight for some time, you have an entirely different problem.

A word of caution again: don't try to swim ashore for help unless the beach is very close and you are certain that you can reach it with plenty to spare. The shore is always farther away than it appears under these circumstances. It is better to lash oneself to the boat and wait for help than it is to drown on a hopeless mission.

The sailor on the near side of this capsized boat is getting the mainsail off the mast while his companion stands on the centerboard preparing to swing the boat upright.

So what to do? Round up the equipment that floated out of the boat (paddles, cushions, boxes and the like), lash it together. Try to right the boat, bail it out and then sail or paddle to shore. If you are in critical need of help and your flares survived the capsize (they should be waterproof), fire them.

Righting a capsized centerboard sailboat is by no means a complicated procedure, and the instances of boats being righted and bailed, the sails being re-set and the race resumed are numerous.

When a centerboard boat is knocked over, it usually winds up with one side submerged, the other sticking out of the water and the mast and sail lying on the surface. To get the boat up, the first thing to do is take the sails down. Someone has to swim to where the halyards are cleated, cast them off and then work the sails down the jibstay and the mast. When they have been secured with their sheets or other line, the next step is to get the centerboard down if it isn't already in that position. Then the crew should stand on the centerboard, heave down on the upper rail and swing the boat upright. Once she is up, it is a matter of getting the water out of her. A bailing scoop or can—provided it didn't go adrift in the capsize—or pump—the same contingency—will do the trick. If you lost these items, then vigorous scooping with cupped hands is your method. It takes longer and is more tiring, but it will get the water down to a level where it is safe to bend sail on again.

And when it is over, remember what caused the flip and *don't* do it again.

CHAPTER 3

Boat Handling and Seamanship

THE mark of a good seaman is the manner in which he handles himself in and around a boat: how he gets aboard, how he loads it, how he gets underway, how he comes alongside, how he picks up a mooring and how he does a dozen other things which the "savvy" boating enthusiast does right and does automatically.

Good boat habits are largely a matter of good training. Learn how to do everything the right, the seamanlike way, and you will be a stranger to trouble. No one will refer to you derisively as a landlubber or hacker. The boating fraternity is a critical group, one that reserves its approval for the competent. It has no time for a bungler.

BOARDING AND LOADING

For instructional purposes let's start with getting into a boat—any small outboard craft. What applies to a boat of this type applies as well to rowboats and small centerboard sailing craft at this stage of the lesson.

When boarding from a float or low pier, step aboard as nearly amidships (the center) as possible, keeping your weight low and using your hands on the gunwales (sides) for balance. If the boat is well below the pier level, extra care is required. Step down to the bow deck if there is one; the distance to it is appreciably less than the distance to the floorboards. Unless you are eager to put a hole through the bottom of the boat, hurt yourself or give an extemporaneous aquatic exhibition, *don't jump* into the boat. Keep the dock lines taut, or have someone steady the boat for you when you embark.

If you have packages and gear to get aboard, don't try to carry them; keep your hands free; you'll need them. After you are in the boat, have someone hand the bags and bundles to you, or reach back to the float for them.

Evinrude Boating Foundation

How not to board a boat

Embarking from the beach is a different operation. Get your gear aboard first, launch the boat stern foremost and then climb in over the bow.

Now for rigging the motor. If you are alone, lay the engine on the float or wharf where you can reach it easily after you are in the boat. Take a firm grip on the motor, swing it directly onto the transom so that the bracket bolts (which you have pre-adjusted to the proper gap) can be quickly tightened. Set up on the bracket screws as hard as you can by hand and then rig your insurance. This is a line or chain passed through a hole in the motor bracket, or around it, and then secured to the stern lifting ring. If your boat has no lifting ring, make the line or chain fast around the transom knee which is, or should be, a good, solid piece of construction. It doesn't matter much just how you do it, so long as you have some such safety device to keep your motor from going overboard if it works loose. If you don't have such a rig then you can look forward to diving in search of the motor, or tiresome dragging for it with a grapnel.

Now you are almost ready to go—the engine is secured in place, gear and gas tanks are aboard. The next step is embarkation of passengers. Don't overcrowd your boat. The newspapers, reporting holiday casualties, all too often report drownings resulting directly from boat overloading.

A boat will only hold so many persons safely and the number of seats is not an accurate indication of its capacity. Most of the modern outboard boats have an Outboard Boating Club plaque which states how many passengers or pounds it is built to carry. Capacity is calculated on the basis of 12 cubic feet of space for each 150 pound passenger. If there is no OBC plaque, do a little simple arithmetic for yourself. An overloaded boat, whether the load be passengers or packages, is in grave danger of swamping in rough water, or in the wake of a passing motor boat. Don't take chances with human life.

Too much weight forward not only reduces speed and risks burying the bow in a wave but also causes cavitation.

Your passengers should be seated so that the boat is in proper "trim", or balance; not down by the stern with the bow in the air or vice versa, and not with one side appreciably lower than the other. Once seated, your passengers should remain so. Don't allow them to stand or change seats until you have throttled down to very low speed, or stopped. You will learn from experience how best to place your passengers, and when you master the knack of trimming your little ship you will discover that she performs better with the weight properly distributed. Nowhere, incidentally, is this more true than in a small, light displacement sailboat. Watch the consistent winners and note how, as much as wind and weather will permit, they keep their boats sailing on their lines.

Today's boats that are built especially for use with outboard engines have transoms 15 or 20 inches high and set at an angle of 12 degrees outward from the keel. Some have a space cut out of the transom especially for the motor. Hence it behooves the boatman to be sure when he is setting his motor that it is in the proper running position—the drive shaft straight up and down, not canted in toward the boat or angled away from it.

If the drive unit is too close to the boat, it will influence the boat to run by the bow—that is, with its nose down and tending to dig in. You can imagine how difficult this would make steering. If the shaft is tilted too far from the transom, the stern will squat, the bow come up and the boat will have a tendency to "porpoise" and pound.

Ever hear of cavitation? Well, you will as long as you are around outboard motors. What happens when you race an automobile engine with the clutch disengaged? Sound and fury, no progress. Much the same occurs when you get cavitation with an outboard motor. One of the chief causes of cavitation is too high a transom, which brings the propeller too close to the surface where it spins through badly disturbed water and doesn't get a real "bite" in it. Cutting a notch in the transom where the bracket fits will often cure this difficulty.

The same principle of weight distribution that governs passenger seating applies to the loading of supplies, equipment and other gear. Never forget the old seaman's adage: "A place for everything and everything in its place." Nothing is quite so lubberly, quite so unseamanlike, as a boat in which all manner of things are lying about loose in the bilges and on the floor boards or seats. Having gear adrift like this is dangerous as well as a good way to hasten the deterioration and loss of equipment. If your boat doesn't have stowage lockers in the bow, under the stern seat or any other seat, it would be wise to build them. There is no such thing on a boat as too much locker space.

GETTING UNDERWAY

Having set the motor securely and properly, trimmed ship and stowed gear, we are now ready to get started on the day's trip. Having followed the instructions in the engine manual—there's one with every engine—you have the proper mixture of oil and gasoline in the tanks and the fuel line connections have been made. It is time to start the motor. Again consult the handbook. It was written by the motor manufacturer and he knows how his product works.

If the engine has a gear shift, you have it set in neutral and have not cast off the dock lines; that can wait until the engine is running. If the engine is not of the gear shift type, then you did not let go the mooring lines until you were ready to pull the starting cord and you didn't yank on it until you had headed the bow toward open water. If you were starting from a beach, you pushed the boat out far enough for the engine to be swung down in operating position before beginning the starting routine. Make sure that there is enough water for the propeller to clear the bottom. A mistake here can mean a sheared propeller pin at least and perhaps a bent blade.

When you are leaving a float or pier, don't push your tiller or spin your wheel so far in one direction that the stern swings sharply against the obstruction when you begin to move. Outboard boats do not steer like bicycles or automobiles. Those vehicles follow their front wheels. In boats, which have their steering mechanism (rudder) aft, the stern responds to the steering impulse first and in the opposite direction from that which the bow is going to take. So in close quarters, give your stern room enough to swing, and save your paint job.

Once underway, there are two basic rules to observe:

1. Keep the boat under control; don't run at high speed where sudden turns or stops might become necessary.

2. Always be alert; keep an eye on other boats, watch for driftwood (it's bad for lower units and, sometimes, bottoms), shoal spots, buoys and other obstructions.

These are the things that you will do instinctively when you become a good seaman, and being a good seaman is at least half of the fun of boating whether you do it in sail or under power.

The cut of a good boat handler's jib is revealed to onlookers (and there always seems to be a large, critical gallery present when things go wrong) by the manner in which he picks up a mooring or comes alongside a landing. We are assuming here, of course, that the boat is not going to be beached.

LANDING AND MOORING

A good landing requires control of the boat, a knowledge of its idiosyncrasies, and awareness of what effect the wind and current, if any, will have on the boat's behavior. In tidal waters or streams where there is noticeable current, it is best to make up-tide or upstream landings unless the wind is so strong and from such a direction that it will more than offset the effect of the current. Where current or tide movement do not have to be taken into account, make your landing with bow in the wind if possible. A glance at flags ashore or on nearby boats will give you the wind direction; a look at the way a buoy is streaming, or the way other boats are lying to their moorings, will tell you the direction in which the current is setting.

Only a landlubber, or an incorrigible hot rodder, would come in for a landing at high speed and at right angles to the float or pier. Any show-off in this department is running the risk of incurring a big shipyard bill and, what is infinitely worse, injuring someone. Heading for a beach, of course, you have no choice but to go right for it, but you do it slowly, swinging your engine up before the lower unit strikes bottom.

Now let's have the procedure for making a good landing. Suppose, for example, that you are heading downstream with the current and there is no breeze to speak of, and the float you want is on the left bank. When you are abreast of the landing place, throttle the motor down and begin an easy left turn. When you are below the float, head upstream in such a way as to bring the starboard side of your boat parallel to the outside edge of the float and a foot or so away from it. When your bow passes the downstream end of the float, stop the engine or put it into neutral, flip the fenders over the rail nearest the float and steer the boat gently alongside. You can hold onto the float until someone takes your bow line, or step ashore with it yourself.

The same principles of speed and approach apply to picking up a mooring buoy in an anchorage. One of your passengers (or crew in the case of a sailboat) can lean over the bow and seize

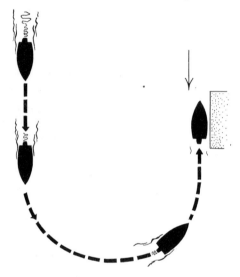

Correct approach to a landing with the boat heading into the dominant wind or current as it comes alongside the pier

the pick-up buoy as you come slowly up to it, informing you by hand signals whether you need to come more left, or right, or keep going ahead to nail it. If you're alone, it is best to run just a little way beyond the buoy so that you can grab it from the cockpit and then lead it forward for securing.

The making fast of a boat to wharf, pier or float depends on what there is present in the way of bollards, cleats or rings for your mooring lines to pass around, over or through. All places normally used for boat landings are, or should be, equipped with one or another.

Floats usually are fitted with cleats and/or rings, and sometimes these floats are held in place by stakes or pilings which are handy projections for making fast the shore end of your lines. Wharves and piers may have metal rings, wooden or metal cleats and wooden or metal bollards. It all depends on the principal use to which the wharf or pier is put. You will note that the word "dock" has not been used here to denote a facility to which boats may be made fast. "Dock" is probably the most incorrectly used word in boating, being used as a synonym for wharf or pier. It isn't. A dock, strictly speaking, is the water space between two piers and the shore. Thus you can put a ship into a dock but you cannot very well moor to one unless it is a dry dock of either the floating or gate variety.

Mooring alongside can be simplified by having eye splices in one end of the bow and stern lines. Pass that end ashore to be slipped over a cleat or bollard and take up the slack on board. When mooring to a ring, the eye can be passed through it, the bitter end of the line reeved through the eye and then led back on board to be secured to the bow or stern cleat as the case may be. If there are no eye splices in your lines, a couple of figure eights around a cleat with a final half hitch to lock the line in place will do well. For securing to bollards, piles, or stakes, a round turn and two half hitches will suffice in quiet water where there is no great strain on the line, but a clove hitch or bowline would be safer; they don't work loose.

If there is no wind or current to carry the stern away from the landing, the bow line will do for short periods alongside, but it is better practice to have the stern line out, too.

When making fast to a wharf or pier in tidal waters, be sure to leave enough slack in the lines to allow for rise and fall of the tide. If you have everything tight at high tide you could very well pull the deck cleats out by their roots when the tide drops, or have your boat suspended in mid-air if cleat and line don't give way. If you must tie up to a pier whose pilings are weed and barnacle encrusted, give a thought to your boat's topsides by rigging a wooden fender or board fore and aft so that its outer face makes contact with the piling and the inner side rests against a battery of rubber or plastic fenders strung along the side of the boat. This is a good rig, too, for use in canal and river locks.

BENDING ON SAIL

Much of what has gone before in this chapter was meant for the newcomer to outboarding. Many of those rules of sea-going procedure apply just as well to sailboats; but there are differences, too, simply because of the difference in motive power.

The knack of getting on board, stowing gear, trimming ship and such is the same, virtually, for one as the other. But getting a sailboat under way is something else again—no flip of a switch, push on the gear control and off you go.

For the purposes of discussion let us assume that a crew of two is about to go for a sail in a 16-foot centerboard sloop, a type which abounds on America's waterways, fresh or salt. The boat is swinging from her mooring and her complement has just come aboard with sail bags, water jug, ditty bag and lunch box.

The first thing to do is to stow the lunch and water supply out of the way. Keep the ditty bag handy if it contains pliers and marlinspike. Then it will be a good idea to lower the centerboard—the plate of iron, bronze, wood or fiberglass that is housed in a "trunk" in the cockpit.

With the board down, the boat will have more stability while you are moving around in her doing the pre-sailing chores. Besides, if you lower the board before you do anything else you won't be embarrassed when you get underway to discover that you had forgotten all about it.

The next job is to reeve the jibsheets, one on each side, running them through the blocks which will be shackled to the clew (the rear lower corner) of the jib and then through the fairleads on the deck to their proper cleats. Don't cleat them; leave plenty of slack for the operations to come.

Now to the mainsail. It may be one of two kinds: built to fit into slots cut into the mast and boom, or fitted with slides that run along tracks screwed to the upper side of the boom and the after side of the mast. In either case, get the foot of the sail on the boom first, secure the tack (forward end) fitting, and then pull the sail out along the foot, fit the clew cringle (the ring in the after end of the sail) into the outhaul and set up on this until the sail is properly taut.

Before hoisting the main, there are three important jobs to do: slip the battens (thin slats of wood that fit into pockets in the sail to give firmness to its after edge, or leach) into their pockets and tie them in firmly with a double square knot, unless your sail is made with the kind of pockets that need no tie; cast off the tiller lashings, and then see that the mainsheet (the line which controls the trim of the mainsail) is free for running through its blocks.

With the boom free of the restraint imposed by the taut mainsheet which held it into the boom crutch, or rest, it will either lift itself out of the crutch when the main is hoisted, or it can be lifted out by hand. Having the tiller free assures that if the mainsail should fill while being hoisted, the boat won't begin charging around the mooring, or threaten to capsize.

Now it is time to run the mainsail up the mast, one sailor guiding the luff rope (the rope to which the leading edge of the sail is sewn) into the slot, or fitting the slides onto the track as the case may be, while the other mans the halyard (the line used to hoist the sail). It is assumed that before you began hoisting you took pains to shackle the main halyard to the head (top) of the sail. If you didn't, the sail wouldn't go up but the halyard would and you'd have the devil's own time getting it down again.

When the main is two-blocked (as high as it will go), secure the halyard on its proper cleat. Some lock it with a half hitch, other equally good seamen do not; they feel that it hampers clearing the halyard and letting it go on the run in the event that the sail has to be doused in a hurry—in a squall for instance. Now that the main is up, get rid of the boom crutch. Stow it under the deck; you won't need it until you're back at the mooring.

On most boats, the fitting by which the boom is attached to the mast (the fitting is called the gooseneck) is in a slide so that it can be raised or lowered a few inches on the spar and thus ease or increase the tension on the luff of the mainsail. The gooseneck is controlled by a piece of line called a downhaul which is secured to the underside of the fitting and then led through a block on deck to a cleat. The downhaul lanyard is kept loose until the main is hoisted then it is hauled down until the luff is adjusted (not too hard in light weather), or the boom reaches the black band painted on the mast. The band is used by some racing classes to designate the lower limit at which the boom can be set.

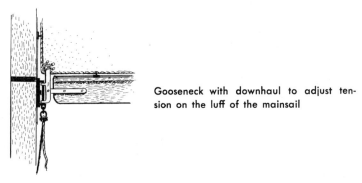

Gooseneck with downhaul to adjust tension on the luff of the mainsail

Now for the jib, or headsail, set forward of the mast. Secure the tack, or lower forward corner of the sail, to its fitting on the deck near the stemhead, which is as far forward as the boat goes. There is either a snapshackle or pin shackle there for this purpose. Hank the jib to the jibstay—that is, clip the snaphooks along its leading edge onto the wire stay that runs from the masthead, or a short distance below it, to the stemhead. Start with the hank nearest the tack and work up, being careful not to get any twists into the sail.

After the jib is hanked on, attach the jibsheets (make sure that they are free) by shackling their blocks to the clew. Next, shackle the jib halyard to the head of the sail and hoist away. Sweat the halyard up tight, because a jib whose leading edge is a series of scallops is a very inefficient sail, particularly on the wind. We are assuming here that the jib battens are, as in the case of many small jibs, sewn into the sail. If not, then they must be slipped into their pockets and, if necessary, tied in before the sail is hoisted.

The sailor has fitted the slides onto the tracks of the mast and the boom, secured the outhaul on the after end of the boom, and shackled the main halyard to the head of the sail. The sail is now ready to hoist.

The crew holds the jib against the wind on the starboard side to help push the boat's head off to port.

THE SAILBOAT GETS UNDERWAY

Now the sails are bent on, luffing gently in the breeze as the boat lies head to wind. You're ready to leave the mooring. The helmsman must decide which tack he wants to take to get away. This decision will be guided by the amount of sailing room around the mooring, or where he wishes to go. A boat is on the port tack when its main boom is to starboard and the wind is coming over the port side; on the starboard tack when the sails are set to port and the wind is coming over the starboard side.

Let us suppose that the man at the helm has decided to sail off on the starboard tack. The crew goes forward, takes the mooring line off the bow cleat and holds it in one hand while, with the other, he backs the jib to starboard, a maneuver carried out by grasping the jib by its clew (lower after corner) and holding it out against the wind on the starboard side. With the jib in this position, the wind will push the boat's head off to port and impel it forward a little. When the bow is around and there is way on the boat, the crew lets the mooring line and pick-up buoy go overboard, releases the jib clew and immediately trims (hauls in) the jibsheet on the port, or lee, side (the one opposite to that from which the wind is blowing) and sets the jib for sailing on the starboard tack.

The helmsman, meanwhile, has been doing his share to get the boat moving in the desired direction. He has helped the bow to fall away to port by pushing the tiller to starboard (tillers work opposite to steering wheels) and, as the boat gathered way, eased the tiller back toward amidships, and trimmed the mainsheet to the proper point for the course to be sailed.

Earlier in this chapter something was said about balance, or trim. It is vital to the performance of small, light sailboats, particularly those of the centerboard type. Generally speaking, weight should be kept amidships so that the boat is on her designed lines and not nose heavy, as airplane pilots say, or dragging her stern. So much for fore and aft trim. In any worthwhile breeze, sailboats heel, that is, lean away from the wind which causes the change in angle from the perpendicular by its pressure against the sails.

A certain amount of heel, enough to lift the weather chine (the joint where topsides and bottom meet in a flat or vee-bottom boat) out of water, is good. It reduces the amount of wetted surface thereby reducing skin friction and helping the speed a little. Too much heel causes the boat to slide off to leeward because the centerboard is no longer at the proper angle to do its best work. Much too much heel causes capsizes.

How to counterbalance too much heel? Simple. The crew (and, in this case, the helmsman is included) sits on the weather deck or rail (the weather side is the one from which the wind is coming, and, if your boat is heeling, it will be the high side). If just sitting on the deck or rail doesn't bring the boat down to her lines, then the crew "hikes"—leans back and out to get its weight where it will be most effective. If the wind is puffy, or gusty, the heavier puffs can be counteracted by a combination of hiking and the easing of the main sheet to allow the mainsail to luff, or shake, until the puff has passed.

At this stage we have the boat sailing and properly trimmed on the starboard tack. Our destination, however, is to windward, the direction from which the wind is blowing.

SAILING FUNDAMENTALS

Except in extremely heavy weather, motor boats can proceed about their business without much thought of wind direction until coming alongside, or making a mooring. Not so with sailing craft. You just can't aim one of those into the wind and go anywhere except perhaps backwards. The average small sailboat cannot sail much closer to the wind than 45 degrees, especially if there is any chop to keep knocking the bow off. Therefore the sailboat must proceed upwind by a series of tacks, or changes in heading, sailing first on one tack and then the other until the destination is achieved, or the wind shifts.

So now it is time to come about onto the port tack. The routine is simple. The helmsman says: "Ready about!" as a notice to the crew that he is going to tack. Next he says: "Hard-a-lee!" and pushes the tiller toward the lee side of the boat. In this case, because we're on the starboard tack, he shoves the tiller, sometimes called the stick, down to port. As he does so, both he and the crew move across the boat to the other side; the crew letting go the jibsheet on the lee or port side and trimming it in as the sail comes around to the other side of the mast. The mainsail takes care of itself because its sheet is led through a block which slides along a track or traveler set athwartships on the stern deck. Nothing has to be done to the centerboard; it stays down.

After tacking, the helmsman sails his boat wide (not too close to the wind) until she regains full headway before bringing her back to her 45 degree angle to the wind.

Angle to the breeze in which the boat is moving can be determind with the help of telltales in the form of strips of colored ribbon, or knitting yarn, tied well up on the shrouds. In boating, shrouds are not sheets in which corpses are wrapped; they are the wire side stays which support the mast.

Jib and mainsail, when trimmed properly with relation to each other, are sometimes said to be "married" which, in this instance at least, means harmoniously adjusted. This situation obtains when neither is trimmed too flat (in too hard) or not enough (out too far), but just right. When the mainsail luffs, one of three things can be wrong: (1) the helmsman is "pinching" the boat, sailing too high or close to the wind, or (2) the mainsail isn't trimmed flat enough, or (3) the jib is trimmed too flat and is backwinding the main.

When the jib luffs, that is, when its entering edge flutters, either it isn't trimmed in enough, or the helmsman has let the boat come up too high. That is why, when he is taking a boat to windward, the good helmsman keeps his eyes on the luff of his jib, keeping it full but not so much so that he is sailing too far off the wind. A glance at the telltales now and then is a help, too.

Reaching, or sailing across the wind, is perhaps the easiest point of sailing. You set the sails at the proper angle for the course and simply steer for the predetermined place. Reaching breezes were called "soldier's breezes" by old shellbacks because they felt that everything was so easy that even a soldier could

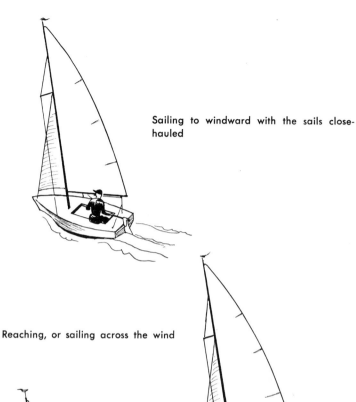

Sailing to windward with the sails close-hauled

Reaching, or sailing across the wind

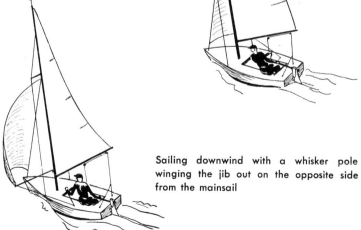

Sailing downwind with a whisker pole winging the jib out on the opposite side from the mainsail

steer more or less well in them. Reaching is also the fastest point of sailing, because sails are eased and the angle to the wind is not acute.

A boat is on a close reach when the wind is forward of the beam, on a beam reach when the wind is abeam, and on a broad reach when the wind is abaft the beam.

When the wind is astern or nearly so—off one quarter (side of the stern) or the other—a boat sails downwind, or to leeward, or, as some sailors call it, downhill. With the wind aft, the mainsheet is allowed to run until the main boom is square to the breeze thus presenting the maximum sail surface to the wind. The jib is useless with the wind dead aft because it is blanketed by the mainsail; useless, that is, unless someone stands up there holding the clew out to windward, or you have a stick called a whisker pole to do the job. The whisker pole has sort of a hook in each end; one fits into the clew of the jib and the other into an eye screwed into the fore side of the mast. Thus the whisker pole holds the jib out square to the wind and adds its sail area to the task of moving the boat. It adds a little horsepower, so to speak.

The whisker pole is a normal item of equipment on small racing sailboats which do not have spinnakers—the large, light, balloon-like sails used for off-the-wind sailing. Setting, trimming and handling them requires a certain amount of skill and training, and is something not to be tackled until the basic sailing techniques have been well learned.

Sailing downwind is a matter of letting the main boom go as far forward as it will go without causing the leading edge of the mainsail to luff, or shake, and steering steadily. Careless steering, especially if there is any sea running, can result in an extemporaneous, or "North River" jibe, an event which could (1) result in giving the crew a hard knock on the noggin as the boom unexpectedly swings across the boat, or (2) damage either boom or shrouds when they come into violent contact, or (3) snap the backstay or capsize the boat if the boom lifted in the process of jibing and caught on the backstay, the wire that runs from the masthead down to the stern.

Intentional jibes are commonplace in sailing to leeward because of necessary changes in course or shifts in wind direction.

The maneuver is simply a matter of swinging the boat's stern so that the wind is brought onto the opposite quarter from where you had been sailing with it. The actual change in direction is slight, enough to get the wind on the end of the boom and swing it over.

Here is how it is done. If you have been sailing with the centerboard up, as most people do unless it is blowing hard, lower it all the way. This act has been preceded by the helmsman's command: "Stand by to jibe!" Having lowered the board, the crew then unships the whisker pole, letting the jib take care of itself for the moment. The helmsman, or his shipmate, then begins to haul in on the mainsheet to keep the boom from lifting when the instant comes for it to swing over to the other side of the boat. The helmsman waits until the boom is almost amidships, cries: "Jibe-O!" and then puts his helm up—pushes the tiller to windward—the opposite move to the one he makes in tacking. The moment the wind takes charge of the mainsail on the new side, the man on the mainsheet lets it run, the tiller is brought back amidships and we're settled down on the new jibe as soon as the whisker pole is rigged and the jibsheets trimmed on what is now the weather side. You can take the centerboard up again now if you like, or leave part of it or all of it down to help with steering.

PICKING UP THE MOORING

Having sailed on the wind (to windward), across it (reaching) and downwind (to leeward), you next pick up the mooring. This is the maneuver which separates the seaman from the lubber and exposes the latter to the derision of onlookers. But even a comparative beginner can accomplish the job well if he does a little thinking beforehand and doesn't panic.

Assuming that current is not the controlling factor, one always approaches the pick-up buoy on a mooring from downwind of it with sails a-luff and just enough way on the boat to reach the buoy; you must not be going so fast that you overrun the buoy, or so slowly that you stop short of it for want of momentum.

Except for the direction from which you make your approach,

Picking up a mooring

there isn't any hard and fast rule for picking up a mooring because so many factors enter into the operation:

Strength and direction of current, if any.
Water surface; smooth or choppy.
How the boat carries its way when head to wind; losing momentum
    slowly and gradually, or stopping quickly.
Wind velocity, and direction with relation to the mooring.
Is the mooring area clear, or crowded?

All of these have to be taken into consideration and your maneuver carried out accordingly.

Obviously you would "shoot" for the buoy—swing the boat
into the eye of the wind and aim for the buoy with sails luffing—
sooner in light air and a foul current than you would if you had
the current running with you, and a good breeze. Your boat will
carry its way longer in smooth water than it will heading into a
sharp chop. If you make your approach by running before a
fresh breeze and then swing up to the buoy, the boat will be
going faster than if you had had to beat (work to windward) up
to the mooring.

If your boat handles well under mainsail alone it is a good
plan to get the jib down, off the stay and into its bag before you

come in for the mooring. That leaves the foredeck clear for the person who has to lie out there on his stomach to reach for the pick-up buoy, snatch it out of the water, lead the mooring pennant through the the bow chock and then secure it on the cleat. It also eliminates the possibility of the jib getting soiled from contact with a muddy mooring line.

SECURING THE BOAT

As soon as the mooring is fast, the mainsail should come down. Follow this procedure: the helmsman sets the boom crutch in place, puts the main boom into it and hauls the mainsheet tight and cleats it, thus assuring that the boom will not go adrift; the crew, first having made certain that the main halyard is free to run, lowers away the mainsail, helping it along, if it is in a slotted spar, by pulling downward on the luff. That bit about making certain that the halyard is free for running is important. Nothing looks quite so silly quite so unseamanlike, as the main halyard up the mast in knots and bunches. An exhibition like this usually results from either slovenly handling of the line, letting the halyard go in too much of a hurry, or dropping the coiled sheet so that it unwinds from underneath the coil instead of from on top.

Now for securing the little ship. Never go ashore and leave everything higgledy-piggledy on board. It not only looks, and is, lubberly, but it isn't good for the gear. First take the battens out of the sail and stow them either in little slings rigged under the deck for that purpose, or slide them through the space behind a couple of deck supports. If you'd rather take them ashore, tie them in a bundle with a short piece of line. Next let the mainsail go from the outhaul and tack fittings, pull it forward and out of the boom slot, or off the boom track, and then stuff it into its bag. If it is wet it can be spread out on the lawn or clothesline ashore to dry. The synthetics from which most sails are made these days dry quickly and there is scant danger of the mildew that has always been a threat to cotton sails. If there is salt in main or jib it can be washed out with a fresh water hose or by dunking the sails in a wash tub.

The main halyard, after being unshackled from the sail, can be led to the outhaul, shackled to it, and then pulled snug so that it doesn't hang loose. The best place for the business end of the jib halyard is the jib tack fitting on the foredeck, then it, too, can be snugged up. Halyards should be coiled evenly in a clockwise direction and hung from their cleats by a loop formed by passing the last coil through and over the entire coil twice as a sort of lock. Unreeve the jibsheets, coil them. and stow them in the bag with the jib. If you prefer to leave them aboard, hang the coil on a hook under the deck out of the weather. Coil the mainsheet and secure it in the same manner as the halyards. The tiller should be set amidships. You can have a permanent rig for this: a piece of light line that can be knotted or spliced into an eye screw in a frame about even with the head of the tiller, clove hitched around the tiller and then cleated under the deck on the other side of the boat. The tiller lashed in this fashion holds the rudder steady amidships and keeps the boat from slewing around at its mooring.

If you have shipped any water into the boat in the course of your sailing excursion, get it out with bailing can and sponge. The next time you get aboard you won't want to step into a mess of water slopping about on the floorboards. Now haul the centerboard up and secure its pennant (the line by which it is raised and lowered) to its cleat.

Gather the sail bags, luncheon box and water jug together in the cockpit, take one good check-up look-around to see whether you have forgotten to do anything, and then signal the tender. You're ready to go ashore.

CHAPTER 4

Customs and Rules of the Road

THE good boatman is, afloat at least, a better than average citizen. He is courteous, thoughtful and law-abiding; he observes the traditions of the sea, and carries out his responsibilities to the boating community. He puts a great deal into his sport and is rewarded in proportion.

In some respects, he is like the motorist who goes out of his way to give other drivers and the pedestrians a break. He knows the traffic laws (in his case, the Rules of the Road) and obeys them meticulously. In the nautical equivalent of traffic jams and congested intersections he uses his common sense; he avoids getting himself into positions where, although he legally has the right of way, it is difficult or impossible for the other person or persons involved to grant him what the law requires. He displays good "road manners" and handles his boat with the thought that others have the same right to the water as he.

Small motor boats and sailing craft have the same responsibility for observing the Rules of the Road as large motor yachts, ocean-going liners and lake freighters. Sea laws, and their river and lake counterparts, apply to all who venture afloat, whether the aim is commercial or the seeking of pleasure.

For reasons which are not apparent to anyone who has made a study of navigation laws, there are no less than four different sets of major nautical rules with which the American boating devotee must be concerned:

41

International Rules: for ocean waters, the great sea highways.

Inland Rules: for all waters within the U.S. (except lakes wholly within the boundaries and jurisdiction of a state) and along its coasts not subject to special rules such as the

Western River Rules: for the Mississippi River, the Red River of the North and their tributaries, and the

Great Lakes Rules: for the Great Lakes and their connecting and tributary waters.

These regulations cover the right of way, lights, and sound signals. In addition to the foregoing laws of wide application there are, in too many parts of the United States, purely local rules concerning speed and hours of operation. The thing to do, of course, is to find out in advance what is expected of you as a boatman before you venture into unfamiliar territory. If you are planning to operate in an area covered by one or more of the major sets of rules listed above, you can get the official Coast Guard motorboat pamphlets from Coast Guard headquarters in Washington, or one of the many Coast Guard Marine Inspection offices located in major port cities.

RULES OF THE ROAD

There are, however, a few simple, fundamental Rules of the Road which, with very minor exceptions, apply everywhere. They should be familiar to and observed by all who go afloat for their fun. Here they are:

1. *Meeting.* When two power vessels approach each other head on, each steers to starboard (bears right) so as to pass port side to port side. In the Great Lakes and on certain rivers where there are channels with strong currents, the vessel going downstream, or down-current, has the right of way over the one which has the current against it. The reason for this is that it is easier to control a vessel stemming the current than it is to steer one being swept along by the current.

2. *Overtaking.* When one boat is overtaking another, the overtaken boat has the right of way. That simply means that, while the overtaken boat holds its course and speed, the one doing the overtaking keeps clear. However, if a small, shoal draft boat is being overtaken in a narrow channel by a larger, deeper

draft vessel, it will be easy for the small boat to swing to the side of the channel and let the big fellow have the deep water. This is one of the situations in which courtesy and common sense take precedence over insistence on right of way.

3. *Crossing.* A motorboat which has another boat in its so-called danger zone (from dead ahead to two points abaft the starboard beam—which roughly translated means coming from your right) must give way to it by altering course so as to pass astern (behind), by slowing, or, if necessary, stopping or reversing. By the same token, if there is a boat approaching your port side (coming from your left) you are the privileged skipper and have right of way.

4. *Leaving Slips, Wharves and Piers.* Boats coming out of slips and basins into open water, or leaving berths at piers and wharves, have no rights until they are entirely clear. Therefore, they proceed with caution and at low speed, and blow a long blast on the whistle as a warning to other craft.

5. *Sailboats* always have the right of way over power boats except in the unlikely situation of a boat under sail overtaking one under power. Courtesy also requires that motorboats give a wide berth to sailing craft engaged in a race. If a motorboat does have to pass close to a sailboat, it should do so slowly and on the leeward side (the side on which the sailboat is carrying its main boom) so as to cause the least possible disturbance from its wake.

Among themselves, sailboats have a code of their own. In racing, a boat on the starboard tack always has right of way over one on the port tack except at turning marks where the inside boat has the right to room to accomplish its rounding of the buoy. When boats are sailing on the same tack, the windward boat is obligated to keep clear. In overtaking situations, the overtaken yacht has the right of way. The International Rules of the Road at sea are at variance with the racing rules in that a vessel running before the wind must keep out of the way of vessels sailing close hauled, but there are so few sailing vessels on the high seas today that the matter is largely academic.

6. *Fishing Boats,* whether anchored or underway, with nets, lines and trawls out, have the right of way because their maneuverability is restricted. Give fishing parties a break; don't try to

see how close you can come to them. And remember, you are liable for whatever damage you cause with your wake.

7. *Tows.* Although under certain circumstances power boats have the right of way over tugs with barges in tow, it is not only good manners but sound seamanship to yield the right of way. A motorboat is much handier than a tug with a string of barges.

8. *Accidents.* In cases of collision, capsize, fire and other serious accidents, it is the duty of boatmen to stand by and render all possible assistance. It is not only a tradition of the sea—and one as old as the sea itself—that mariners always go to the aid of those in distress, but the federal boating act of 1958, which has been copied by many states, *requires* that the operator of any boat involved in an accident causing death, personal injury or property damage must stop, render assistance and offer identification, notify the authorities, and file a written report of the incident.

The observance of these eight basic rules of the water roads will stamp you as a good boatman. Now for a few "don'ts," "nevers" and "always-es" concerning matters of custom and etiquette. Adherence to this code will stamp you as a better boatman, one who will be welcome in boating society everywhere. Read, mark, learn and inwardly digest the following:

Don't moor your boat to government buoys or local navigation markers except in emergencies.

Don't anchor in a channel or fairway while fishing; you're blocking traffic.

Don't make it impossible for others to use a float or pier by making your boat fast in the only available space and then leaving it there.

Never run fast through an anchorage, or past a float or pier where boats are secured; nautical hot-rodders are as dangerous and as thoroughly detested as their automobile counterparts.

Never anchor so close to another boat that yours might foul the other's anchor line, or swing against it when the tide or wind changes.

Don't land at a private landing except in an emergency, or by invitation. You'll be as unwelcome as those who ignore "private" signs ashore.

Never throw garbage or refuse overboard in harbors, near beaches, or in lakes used for drinking water supply. Some ports provide garbage collection service, others have refuse receptables at their landings.

Never leave the wheel while running in a harbor.

Don't stare at other boating parties or into cruiser cabins. (You wouldn't peek into neighbors' homes if you were ashore, would you?)

Always offer a tow or some spare gasoline to a boat that has broken down, or run out of fuel.

Always keep an alert lookout. It pays dividends in avoiding collisions with other boats and will minimize the danger of your running into drifting objects that could damage your hull or propeller.

Always—yes, always—be considerate of others.

WHISTLE SIGNALS

There will be times when you should use whistle signals and, perhaps, more times when you will need to know their meaning when you hear them. In a meeting situation, one short blast means "I wish to pass you on my port side." Two short blasts mean "I wish to pass you on my starboard side." Three short blasts mean "My engines are going astern." The danger signal under Inland and Western River Rules is four short blasts; on the Great Lakes it is five or more short, rapid toots of the horn.

The vessel which whistles first gains no rights over the other by so doing. If the signal you receive is proper under the circumstances, answer it with the identical signal. If it is wrong, then blow the danger signal and both vessels should stop. Cross signals —that is, when the first boat blows one blast and the other vessel blows two—are forbidden by law. Whistle signals, incidentally, are never given to or by a boat under sail. There is an exception to the no-signals-by-sailboats rule: in fog, a sailboat on the port tack blows two blasts in succession every minute; one on the starboard tack blows one blast at intervals of not more than a minute.

BUOYS

Knowledge of the buoyage system is essential to safe boating. Uncle Sam, state governments and town fathers spend Heaven-alone-knows-how-many hundreds of thousands of dollars a year in building, setting out and maintaining visual aids to navigation in the form of buoys, beacons and lighthouses, and publishing charts (the maritime equivalent of road maps) which show their location with relation to rocks, shoals, hazards, harbor entrances, fairways and the like. Get the charts which apply to the locality in which you are going to do your boating, learn to read them, and govern the movements of your boat accordingly. There is no point in the taxpayers' expending revenue to plant buoys around a reef if you are going to ignore them and pile your boat up on the rocks.

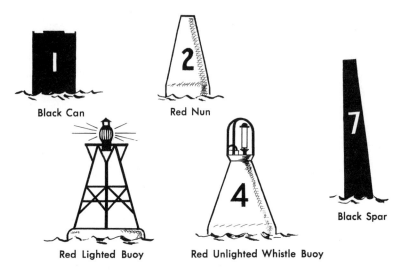

Black Can   Red Nun   Black Spar

Red Lighted Buoy   Red Unlighted Whistle Buoy

Our buoyage system dates back to colonial times. History tells us that as early as 1767 there were buoys of a sort on the Delaware River. Early markers were spars or hollow sheaves of barrel staves, but the history of our buoys is a history of progress and improvement. The first lighted buoy was an oil burner put into service outside New York harbor in 1881. Tall cans and nuns came into use at the turn of the century. Bell buoys which depended upon the roll of the sea to make their clappers ring the bell, appeared in 1885. Now compressed gas activates the striking mechanism. And so it goes until today we are experimenting with automatic radio beacon buoys and other advanced types.

On federal waters, the Coast Guard has the responsibility for placing buoys and keeping them on station and in prime working order. And the buoys and their characteristics are the same whether you are sailing in the Chesapeake or steering a cruiser across Puget Sound.

Some states have their own marking systems for waters wholly within their borders, and counties and municipalities often buoy strictly local waters where there isn't enough traffic to warrant the placing of federally maintained aids to navigation. Some of these local marks are primitive, taking the form of slender stakes or bits of brush. Learning what they mean and what they mark comes under the head of acquiring local knowledge, and very vital knowledge it is, too.

However, most local systems follow the basic rule, the "three r's" of piloting: "red light returning." This is an easy way to remember that when you are approaching a harbor from seaward, all of the red buoys are kept to starboard, or on the right hand. The black buoys, naturally, are then kept to port. Conversely, when you are leaving a harbor, the situation is reversed: red buoys to port, black to starboard.

In the federal system, there are four fundamental types of buoys: nuns, cans, lighted buoys and sound buoys (these include bell, gong and whistle buoys). Nun buoys are conical in shape, are painted red, and carry even numbers. They mark the starboard side of the channel when coming in from sea. Can buoys are black, cylindrical in shape, and carry odd numbers. They mark the port- or left-hand boundary of the channel—when you are coming into a harbor, of course.

Sound and lighted buoys may be painted either color, depending on their use, and sometimes are combined to form lighted bell buoys, and such. The gongs, bells and whistles (the latter are sometimes referred to by seafarers as "hooters" or "groaners"; they do have a mournful sound) are to help navigation in times of poor visibility. Lights serve to facilitate movement by night.

There is system about the lighting, too. Lighted buoys on the port side of a channel (on the way in) have either green or white illumination and may be either fixed or flashing. Those on the starboard side (still heading into the harbor, remember) show either red or white lights. At night, lighted buoys are identifiable by their characteristics, that is, by the type of illumination they display.

The signals can be occulting, quick flashing, group flashing, interrupted flash, or short-long combinations and vary in the frequency of the light's appearance. Thus the mysterious symbols "Fl G 5 sec" alongside a buoy sign on a chart means a flashing green light showing at 5-second intervals.

Once a boatman becomes accustomed to buoys and their reasons for existence, he reads them automatically, much as he reads road signs ashore. After all, buoys are nothing more than the road signs of the sea. For instance, he knows that red and black horizontally striped buoys indicate channel junctions, or middle grounds and obstructions. They may be passed on either hand, but the color of the topmost band indicates on which side the preferred channel lies. Vertically striped black and white buoys indicate to the seaman mid-channel (fairway) points.

There isn't anything difficult or complicated about our system of buoying harbors, wrecks, and hazards of all sorts. It is a very good system and it is a sensible habit to leave channel markers on the proper side even if your boat draws only a little water and there would be plenty to spare if you cut the corner. The buoys were put there for a perfectly good purpose and the good seaman doesn't take chances, or pretend to know more than those whose job it is to put buoys out there for his protection.

In its suggestions for safety in boating, the Coast Guard has this to say about buoys: "Know their meanings—what they mark, and what their peculiar markings indicate. Learn how they should be passed—on which side, whether close aboard or well clear; the significance of their lights, by color and characteristics. And never, never, moor to one. It is a Federal offense for which a penalty of $500 could be imposed."

TIP FROM THE BOS'N

Where can you get charts of your waters or those to which you are going? Here are the answers:

The United States Coast & Geodetic Survey, Washington 25, D.C., makes charts for coastal waters and adjoining navigable rivers; it also compiles current tables and draws tidal current charts. These can be obtained from the Superintendent of Documents, Washington 25, D.C., or from field offices and sales agencies in major ports.

For charts of major inland rivers try the various and numerous district offices of the Corps of Engineers, United States Army.

For charts of the Great Lakes, Lake Champlain, New York state canals, the United States Lake Survey, 630 Federal Bldg., Detroit 26, Michigan, is the source.

CHAPTER 5

Ropes, Knots, and Splices

BESIDES their love of the water and the vessels that scurry about on its surface, devotees of motor boating and those whose enthusiasm finds its expression in sail have something else in common: the need to know about rope and what to do with it.

In the long-gone days of the commercial sailing ship, marlinspike seamanship—tying knots, making splices, fashioning chafing gear and fancy sennit work—was almost a career in itself, but every good sailor was adept at its fundamentals. He had to be; his job, the safety of the ship and even his life, depended on his ability to make the right knot for the right task, and make it quickly and accurately.

Today, only hobbyists and worshippers at the shrine of the traditional display as much virtuosity in the knot tying art as the old-time boatswains. No one needs to know that many different knots any more, or has any practical use for them. Some experts say that you can get by with only three knots: the square (or reef) knot, clove hitch and bowline. Others argue that nine is the minimum for the good seaman. Probably the answer lies somewhere between. If you get fun out of knot tying, it is easy enough to increase your repertory; whole books have been written on the subject.

A WORD ABOUT ROPE

Whether you learn to tie three or thirteen or thirty knots, you should know something about the material from which they are fashioned—rope. You used to find all kinds of rope on pleasure boats, especially sailing craft: manila, linen, cotton, Italian hemp and what not. Nowadays, the emphasis is largely on only three: Manila, nylon and dacron. The synthetics, more expensive initially but longer lasting, stronger by far and more flexible than manila, have just about taken over the cordage department.

They have exceptional resistance to abrasion, run easily through blocks and will not kink or swell when wet. Because they will neither rot nor mildew, nylon and dacron lines can be stowed wet without coming to harm.

Nylon has just about three times the elasticity of manila and linen yacht rope, and for that reason makes excellent anchor rode and docking line. Small, light nylon is used for flag halyards. Dacron has much less stretch, and this stability plus its great strength makes it ideal for sail halyards and sheets. Both nylon and dacron knot and splice nicely, and they untie easily—or at least more easily than ordinary rope—because they do not swell when wet.

Before you tackle the job of learning knots and splices it is best to know a little about how rope is constructed. Standard rope has three strands, each strand made up of a number of yarns twisted together. The lay of a rope is the direction in which the strands are twisted—right or left. Most rope is right laid, that is, the strands spiral upward to the right when a piece is held vertically. Hence yacht cordage is always coiled clockwise, or "with the sun," to obviate kinking and snarling.

Like everything else on a boat, rope needs good care if it is to last a proper lifetime and never let you down in an emergency. Rope deteriorates for a number of reasons. Principal among these is mechanical action, the surface wear and tear, and internal friction between fibers. Running rigging (sheets and halyards) is particularly susceptible because it is always on the move through chocks, blocks and fair leads, and around cleats. That is why only the best rope should be used for these jobs and why sheets and halyards should be reversed (end-for-ended, the sailor calls it) occasionally—this changes the point of wear. There is always a certain amount of friction present when rope is bent over a sheave in a block, and it is this friction which eventually breaks down the fiber of the rope. When this happens, the rope has seen its day.

Deterioration by mechanical action can be reduced in some instances by the proper use of chafing gear—wrapping mooring lines in canvas or covering them with a length of split rubber hose at the point where they run through chocks or hawse holes.

Other causes of rope breakdown are the chemical action of acids and alkalines, and the presence of moulds or insects. Synthetics (nylon and dacron) are far less likely to be damaged from these causes than are ropes of vegetable origin.

Keep ropes clean and free from sand, mud and slime by washing them once in a while in clear water. This will keep grit from working its way inside and acting as a grinding agent to destroy fibers. Rope that is dried on deck and then stowed in a dry, well ventilated locker will not fall victim to dry rot or mildew.

Regular examination of all of your boat's lines is good seamanship. Look for cuts, mildew, dry rot, abraded spots. Don't be satisfied with outward appearance; twist the rope open and look for trouble between the strands. If the inner fibers seem colorless or broken, or if a musty odor greets your inquiring nose, you've got a piece of "dead" rope. Throw it away, or make fenders out of it.

We have been using the word "rope" here the way it has common acceptance ashore. Rope is something the sailor buys in coils or by the pound. Once it gets into use aboard ship, "rope" gives way to certain specific titles: it becomes sheets, halyards, guys, line and rode—sheets for trimming sails, halyards for hoisting them, guys for use with the spinnaker pole, line for docking and myriad odd jobs, rode for the anchor.

The seaman will tell you that there are only nine ropes aboard ship (and he means a really *big* sailing ship) and he lists them as follows: bucket rope, tiller rope, bell rope, man rope, top rope, foot rope, bolt rope, back rope and yard rope. In modern practice you would be lucky to encounter as many as three of them, so be prepared to refer to cordage by its proper name—you can't go far wrong if you call a piece of it "line."

Knots and splices are never as strong as the line itself. A knot may weaken the basic rope by as much as 50 per cent, but a splice has up to 95 per cent of the breaking strength of the line in which it is laid. Knots, you see, have a tendency to lower the resistance of rope fibers to strain. One big cordage company ran a series of tests with certain knots in manila line and came up with the following figures on the percentage of hauling strength of the knot or splice compared with the tensile strength of the rope itself: bowline 50 per cent, square knot 50 per cent, short splice 95 per cent, long splice 90 per cent.

This is one reason why permanent mooring lines are made with eye splices in the ends going ashore, and why eye splices are made around metal thimbles in the end of the anchor rode that is shackled to the anchor ring. Put enough tucks into the splice, do the job well, and a splice won't let you down.

KNOTS

For all practical purposes there are three classifications which cover all the knots a person needs to know whether he depends on Nature to provide the motive power for his boat or whips up a gasoline breeze. They are knots in the end of a rope, knots for tying (bending is the sea-going word) two lines together, and knots for securing a line to a post, tree, spar or ring.

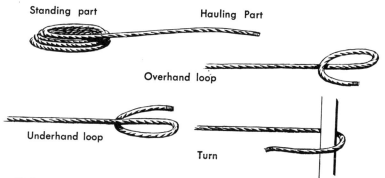

Standing part   Hauling Part

Overhand loop

Underhand loop

Turn

Before we start tying knots let us get squared away on the nomenclature of the art. The *standing part* of a line is that part which is fast, the opposite to the *hauling part*, or free end. The free end is also known as the bitter end. An *overhand loop* is formed by crossing the end *over* the standing part; an *underhand loop* by doing just the opposite. A *turn* is made by passing a line around an object. Whenever two sections of line cross each other in forming a knot, one must go *over* and the other *under*. Mistakes in the over and under sequence in knot tying can result in strange knots, or none at all. When it is formed, a knot is *drawn up*, that is, tightened. This must be done slowly and evenly to insure that all parts of the knot keep their place and shape. Remember, too, that it is as important to fashion a knot so that it will untie quickly as it is to make one that will hold; otherwise in emergency situations you will have to resort to the knife.

Now we'll take up the knots themselves. You can handle most situations with no more than four of them: a figure-of-eight as a stopper to keep a line from running through a block or fairlead; the bowline, which has a wide variety of uses, for forming a loop in the end of a line; the clove hitch, a quick, simple way of securing a line to a bollard, or stake; and the reef or square knot for tying reefs into sails, joining ends of two lines of equal diameter together and securing sail stops. We'll do these four and then add a few embellishments.

 **Reef or Square**

1. *The basic square knot,* sometimes called the sailor's knot by those who don't go afloat. Take two pieces of line, or opposite ends of the same line; pass the left end *over* and *under* the right end. Now curve what has become the left end towards the right. Cross what is now the right end *over* and *under* the left, and draw the knot tight. If you are, or were, a Boy Scout all you have to do is remember the rule of left over right, right over left. Untying a wet reef knot is no picnic, particularly if the line is under strain. To get around this, most sailors, when tying in reefs or securing a sail to the boom with sail stops, form a loop with the second part of the knot (right and over and under the left) instead of pulling the end through. Then, when it comes time to undo the knot, a tug on the end forming the loop casts it loose and the rest is easy.

2. *The figure-of-eight.* Take the end of a line, pass it *under*

and *over* the standing part and then *through* the loop thus formed. Draw it up and you have a good stopper and one easy to untie.

Figure-of-eight

3. *The bowline,* pronounced "bo-lin" the workhorse of knots, can be tied directly around an object, but is generally made up in the hand. Make an *overhand loop* with the end held toward you. Pass the end up *through* the loop then *behind* the standing part

Bowline

and *down through* the loop again. By pulling steadily on the end and standing part you will set up the knot.

4. *The clove hitch.* There are two ways of doing this one. First, make a turn with the line around the post, or stake, or whatever, and then *over* itself. Take a second turn and pull the

Clove hitch

end up *under* the second turn so that it lies between the line and the post. Pull both ends to tighten. For safety's sake, it is a good idea to put a half hitch in the end of the line to keep it from slipping. The hitch is made by passing the end of the line over the standing part and tying an overhand knot in it.

The other method of forming a clove hitch is to make the two loops in the end of the line and drop them over the top of the post. Tighten in the usual manner (taking a strain on standing part and free end) and then put in the half hitch. As a substitute for the clove hitch when securing a dinghy by its painter, or making dock lines fast, some seamen use a couple of round turns and two half hitches. They pass the end of the line around the post twice and then tie the two half hitches around the standing part in the form of a clove hitch.

Now for two useful bends and another hitch. They are not fundamentally essential, but they are nice to know and likely to come in handy, especially when you move into larger boats.

The first of these is the *fisherman's bend*, or *anchor bend*. It is used for tying up to a ring, or for making the anchor line fast to the anchor ring. There are those who prefer the latter method to

Fisherman's or Anchor bend

the eye splice and shackle. You make the fisherman's bend by taking two round turns around the ring, passing the end over the standing part and then between the turns and the ring. Pull it tight, put in another half hitch for security, and there you are.

The *sheet bend*, or *becket bend* (landsmen know it as the weaver's knot) is used for bending (tying, that is) two lines together because it will not slip even if the lines are quite disparate

Sheet or Becket bend

in circumference. If the lines are going to be kept together for any length of time (as in towing, for instance) the free ends of both lines should be stopped down (tied) to the standing parts. To make the sheet bend, first make an overhand loop with the end of one rope. Pass the end of the other rope through the loop thus formed, carry it up behind its standing part then down through the loop again. Draw up by taking a strain on the ends.

The *rolling hitch* can be used for making the end of a line fast to its own standing part without leaving any slack, for bending one line to another, or for making a halyard fast to a stay to keep it away from the mast. It can take a load only in one direction: parallel to the line or spar to which it is fast. Properly made, though, it will not slip, and it is undone easily whether or not under load. This is the way it is made. Take the free end to the standing part, pass it around once and then *between* its own hauling part and the standing part. Then go around again, this

Rolling hitch

time making the turn *below* the one already formed but coming up *between* this turn and the hauling part. This makes the "nip," the point where the pressure comes, and when the hauling part is under load the second turn has to be formed *above* the first turn and then drawn hard in between it and the hauling part. The job is finished off with a half hitch around the hauling part *below* and clear of the first two turns.

Some people call it a hitch; others do not dignify it with such a title, calling it merely a method for belaying a line to a cleat. It is a simple operation, but you'd be surprised how often it is done incorrectly. Do it this way and you won't get into trouble: with the free end, take the slack out of the line and then make a round turn around the base of the cleat; next put two figure eights on the horns of the cleat by (after making the round turn) bringing the free end over one horn, under it and then over and under the other horn. Do this twice and then put another round turn around the base. If the line is an anchor line, or is on a cleat where it could be flogged by a headsail, top off the job with a half hitch over one horn. It can't go adrift that way.

SPLICES

Splices do a better and stronger job than knots and should be used where the joining of two lines, or the making of a loop in one, is to be permanent. There are three basic splices: short,

long and eye. The short splice is used to join two lines permanently, provided they do not have to run through a block or fair
lead. The long splice, which is not so thick (the short one almost
doubles the size of the line), is usually used in halyards and dock
lines. The eye splice puts a permanent loop in the end of a line.

To begin a *short splice,* unlay the strands of both line ends
for a few inches and seize the strand ends, or wrap them with
plastic tape, to keep them from untwisting. Join the ends so that

Short splice

the strands of one rope lie alternately between the strands of the
other. One set of strands can be tied down temporarily to make
things easier. Now the strands of the opposite set are tucked over
and under the strands of the line, and *against* the lay (twist) of
the rope. Pass each tuck over one strand, under the second and
out between the second and third. This, incidentally, is the way
that strands are tucked when making an eye splice.

After one set of strands has been tucked, work the other set
into the opposite line. Take two more tucks with each of the six
strands, trim off the projecting ends (not too close, though), roll
the splice between a foot and the deck, and that's it.

The *long splice* is used when ropes are to be permanently
joined in such a manner that they will run freely through a fair
lead, or block. That is why you see them so often in sheets and

Long splice

halyards. Unlay the strands of both rope ends about four times
as far as required for the short splice (you're going to make more
tucks). Join them as you did in the short splice—one strand of
one line alternating with one of the other. Next unlay one strand

of one rope and in its place lay the *opposite* strand from *the other* rope. The process is repeated for two other strands, but in the *opposite* direction. Four strands thus are accounted for, the other two having been left in the position they took when the ends were first placed together. Instead of tucking the strands against the lay, as we did in the short splice, each tuck in a long splice goes *with* the lay of the rope so that it follows continuously *around the same* strand.

Make plenty of tucks, particularly when working with nylon and dacron. That is slippery stuff. An extra tuck or two won't hurt. You can make a neat finish by tapering the splice. This is done by cutting out a third of the yarns before making the next to the last tuck, and half of the remaining yarns of each strand before making the last tuck.

The *eye splice* is made exactly like the short splice except that it is made with one piece of line. After unlaying the strands in the end to be worked, the end is bent around to form an eye,

Eye splice

and is spliced into the standing part. The splice can be finished and protected by seizing (wrapping marlin tightly around it.)

Practice makes perfect in the fashioning of knots, bends, hitches and splices. Get a couple of short lengths of line and work with them in your spare moments. You will be surprised at how facile you will become in the marlinspike seaman's role.

The mark of a good seaman is the condition of his line. Raveled ends are anathema to him; Irish pennants the hallmark of a lubberly skipper. So he forestalls the possibility of having his lines grow cowstails by seeing that their ends are "whipped," or bound.

There is an easy way to do it—buy a roll of black plastic tape and wrap the stuff around the ends much in the same manner that you would bandage a finger tip. That is the lazy man's way.

The real seaman begins with marline, or spunyarn, or fine yarn, or sail twine. Then he places the end of the twine at the end of the rope and makes a loop. The next step is to wind the twine tightly around both loop and line for at least a distance equal to the rope's diameter. When close to the end of the line, put the winding end through the loop and then pull the end tight until the loop is drawn back out of sight under the coils of whipping. The last step is to snip off the ends. A neat, seamanlike job is finished.

TIP FROM THE BOS'N

"Different ships, different long splices" was the old sailor's way of saying that certain things were done differently on different vessels. When you are a guest or crew on a boat for the first time, find out how its skipper likes his lines coiled and cleated, and whatever special quirks he has in doing things. It will make him happy and save irritation.

CHAPTER 6

Anchors and Anchoring

GOOD ground tackle—the anchor and its appurtenances—is vitally important in boating.

Every boat, motor or sail, needs at least one anchor capable of holding it in bad weather, and plenty of sturdy line to go with it. And if its home berth is not a marina slip, or small boat float, or if it isn't beached between trips, or hauled away by trailer, the boat needs a mooring.

The mooring is its permanent spot in the home anchorage. The nature of the mooring depends on the nature of the anchorage—whether it is crowded or relatively uncrowded, whether it is exposed or sheltered, and what kind of a bottom it has.

Moorings take many forms and most of them do the job satisfactorily. Old railroad car wheels, discarded automobile engine blocks, large buckets of concrete with eyebolts in them—all of these improvisations will do the work of the conventional mushroom anchor under certain conditions. Just find out what has proved to be best in your harbor and go along with that.

It is very comforting, though, to know that when the wind howls and a sea kicks up, your boat is lying to a mooring rig of which a sturdy mushroom is the basis. When a mushroom digs itself into the mud it is mighty hard to move so long as the pull is steady and in one direction, especially if there is a good-sized length of heavy chain between the mushroom and the mooring pennant to dampen the surge when the boat is pitching and tossing.

PRECAUTIONS

How large a mushroom to use, and how much chain and nylon or manila to use with it, again depends on local conditions. In crowded yacht club anchorages where space is at a premium, local regulations specify heavy moorings and short scope. If there is plenty of swinging room available, a lighter anchor and longer pennant are indicated.

Because the safety-minded seaman always errs on the side of extra weight in this department, a fair rule of thumb is ten pounds of mushroom for every foot of overall length of the boat. Thus, if your outboard runabout is 15 feet long or your sailboat 14 feet 10 inches, the mushroom at the bottom of your mooring rig should be a 150-pounder. There will be weight to spare.

As to length of line, it makes a difference what kind of a boat you are going to moor and where. A centerboard sloop moored closed inshore in shoal water shouldn't have too long a line. A heavy motorboat with a high deckhouse or bow that will cause her to take abrupt sheers on windy days, should have an extra allowance. Again a rule of thumb: for scope try four to five times the depth of the water in the mooring area. The greater the scope, the better the chances are of holding.

But don't gamble with your mooring. Have a good anchor for it and, if you are using manila, change the pennant at least every two seasons. In some waters it will be trustworthy only one. Good ground tackle is your best insurance.

ANCHORS

There is a wide and, to the layman, bewildering variety of anchors for other than permanent mooring use. There is, of course, the familiar yacht anchor with a stock that can be folded against the shank before stowing. And there are patented anchors like the Danforth, the Northill and the plow, to say nothing of minor variations thereof, two mushrooms and the grapnel.

The patented anchors are gaining in popularity among boating people because, under most circumstances, they do a better job of holding per pound of weight than the conventional hooks. No one likes to sweat and strain getting a heavy anchor up when a much lighter one would have done the job. No matter which type you use, it is a good idea to have it made up ready for use when you are cruising or making long runs: engines do run out of fuel, engines break down and sailboats run out of wind with the current setting them the wrong way, or into danger.

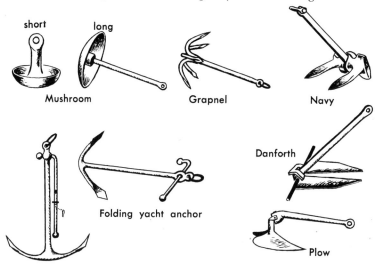

short long

Mushroom Grapnel Navy

Danforth

Folding yacht anchor

Plow

Getting ready is the important part of anchoring and part of getting ready is having the anchor stock in position and locked, the anchor cable either shackled on, or bent on with an anchor bend or a bowline, and the bitter end of the anchor line secured. Believe it or not, there have been instances of fuzzy-minded boatmen dropping anchors overside without first attaching the anchor line, and losing both anchor and rode because they neglected to make the bitter end fast. Blunders like these are not only expensive; they can be dangerous in some situations.

ANCHORING

When you are preparing to anchor, get the mudhook out on deck forward and pile the anchor rode on top of it. If the bitter end is not already secured to a ring, a cleat, or around the mast, then make it fast. Next, coil the anchor rode loosely. When you get to the anchor give it another check to be certain that everything is as it should be at that end. You are now ready to let the anchor go overside at the proper moment.

What is the proper moment? When your boat, headed into wind or current—whichever is the controlling factor—has reached the predetermined anchoring spot, has lost all headway and is beginning to drift backwards.

When you let the anchor go, don't imitate a shot putter. Throwing the hook overside is nothing more or less than an invitation for the anchor to foul itself in the rode—and fouled anchors are notorious for their poor holding qualities. Simply ease the anchor over the side as the boat loses headway and hold it there by the line until it is time to let it go. Do just that; let go of it and gravity will do the rest.

Pay out the line until the hook hits bottom and allow three times the depth to run out before you snub the line on cleat or bit to discover whether the anchor has bitten into the bottom. If it has, the boat's head will swing immediately into the wind or current. If the anchor has not taken hold, you can tell by tugging on the line and feeling the hook still moving on the bottom. Give it more scope before you try again. A sailboat, of course, has to drift back on its anchor to set it. A motorboat can help by going astern slowly on its engines until the hook gets a good bite.

After you are satisfied that the anchor is properly set, pay out anchor line until you have a six-to-one ratio of line to water depth. That should do in all but unusual conditions of sea and wind. However, unless you have anchored where there is not too much swinging room, it is always better to have out too much anchor line than too little.

As soon as you have finished the anchoring job and the boat has settled down, take bearings on marks ashore, or nearby larger boats if you know them to be at permanent moorings. Then, if your position subsequently changes with relation to them, you will know that your anchor is dragging.

When anchoring where the bottom is rocky—your chart or local knowledge will tell you this—be sure to have a trip line on the anchor. It will be a godsend if the anchor sticks down there and shows a reluctance to come up when coaxed. A trip line is easy to rig. When readying the anchor for lowering, make fast around the crown and that end of the shank a reasonably light but strong line. Pay it out with the anchor rode and secure it on deck after you have the anchor set. Or, if you prefer, you can make it fast to a buoy and let it go. You can always pick it up when the time comes and meanwhile it will show you where your anchor lies.

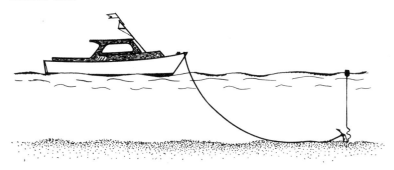

Boat riding at anchor with trip line rigged to help in freeing the anchor if it becomes foul.

If the anchor balks when you heave in on the rode and refuses to budge, a good heave on the trip line usually will lift it out. Motorboats usually can break an anchor out of the bottom simply by going straight ahead after the line has been brought almost up and down.

When a sailboat's anchor is reluctant to come up, it more often than not can be sailed out. This is merely a matter of getting sail on the boat, trimming in the sheets and sailing around the anchor in circles until it breaks loose.

One of the better rope manufacturers in the United States has definite recommendations for ground tackle. Since we are concerned here with only those boats which beginners are likely to have, i.e., reasonably small boats, we shall list only the smaller sizes:

Motorboat under 20 feet: length of anchor cable, 100 feet; diameter, nylon, 3/8-inch; best manila, 1/2-inch; recommended anchor weight, 20 to 35 pounds.

Sailboat under 20 feet: length of anchor cable, 100 feet; diameter, nylon, ⅜-inch; best manila, ½-inch; recommended anchor weight, 30 pounds.

Motorboat 20 to 25 feet: length of anchor cable 100 to 150 feet: diameter, nylon, ⅜-inch light, ½-inch heavy; best manila, ½-inch light, ⅝-inch heavy, recommended anchor weight, 20 pounds for the light anchor, 35 pounds for the heavy. (If you're going to carry only one, use the heavier.)

Sailboat 20 to 25 feet: length of anchor cable, 125 to 200 feet; diameter, nylon, ⅜-inch light, ½-inch heavy; recommended anchor weight, 20 pounds light, 35 pounds heavy. (Again, if you're going to carry only one, use the heavier—be sure.)

Now for an anchoring detail checkoff list:

1. Before anchoring, have some idea of the depth of water; look the anchorage over carefully and decide where you are going to drop the hook. A look at the other boats will tell you how wind and/or tide are affecting them.

2. Look over the anchor and its appurtenances carefully before letting go. And always drop it flukes first.

3. Until the boat has lost headway, never let the anchor go unless it is necessary to do so to avert a grounding or collision.

4. Take ranges as soon as anchored; note them in the log and, if wind or tide are strong, take frequent checks on your bearings.

5. If you are going to lie to your hook overnight, be sure that the line on deck is properly secured and nothing is interfering with the anchor hawser; check to see whether the anchor is dragging.

6. Before turning in for the night, ease out a few inches of anchor line so that a different section is in the chock. Put chafing gear on if you haven't already done so.

7. Allow enough scope for rise and fall in tide, and a possible shift in wind.

CHAPTER 7

Boat, Motor, and Equipment Care

THERE is little that pleases the real sailor more than to have a person whose opinion he respects look at his boat and say: "You certainly keep her shipshape and Bristol fashion."

Pride in his vessel, new or old, expensive or modest—pride in her appearance and the condition of all of her gear and equipment—is characteristic of the seaman.

No one realizes better than he that with the fun of sailing or motor boating goes the responsibility for keeping his boat and everything about her in the very best of condition from stem to stern, truck to keel, rail to rail. He realizes, too, that every hour of labor, every dollar of expense will come back in satisfaction and freedom from trouble.

Slick outward appearance isn't enough. Beauty has to be more than skin deep. Interior finish must be well maintained, rigging kept in top condition, bilges clean and dry, all gear in good working order and properly stowed, and motor tuned for peak performance.

Doing a thorough maintenance job in and out of season is work for the body and the checkbook. But you can add to your boating pleasure and reduce your costs by doing at least part of the labor yourself. Only the well-heeled can afford to leave everything to the shipyard.

It is a fact of boating life that a boat in which competent design, good materials and fine workmanship have been combined will last a lifetime if it is lovingly and intelligently cared for along the way. Conversely, it can become a pitiful hulk in a few years if used too roughly, or neglected. There are few sadder sights than a once handsome craft rotting away for want of attention, and there are few happier pictures for the boat lover to admire than that of a splendid old-timer, shining and sound, reveling in her element like a two-year-old. On Buzzards Bay and Narragansett Bay there are to this day dozens of Herreshoff 12½- and 15-footers that are more than half a century old, and they are still being raced, and raced hard. Furthermore, their asking prices are a great deal higher than their original tags.

How come? Simply a matter of beautifully built boats having had good care down through the years, and by one owner after another.

There isn't anything complicated or difficult about keeping a boat looking—and acting—like new. A turn of a grease cup, a drop of oil, timely and intelligent use of scraper, sandpaper, paint, varnish and scrubbing brush can do wonders along these lines.

Competent advice on hull maintenance is easy to get and costs no more than what it takes to write a letter and mail it to one of the surface coating manufacturers. (We used to say "paint makers," but the continual development of new bases for combining with pigments makes the term rather inadequate.)

Covering a wooden hull used to be a fairly simple process: copper or bronze paint for the bottom, varnish for spars and rails, a good lead for the topsides and more of the same, but a different color, for the decks. The chemists have changed all that in the last few years with their discoveries in the field of resins. Now we have all manner of formulae for the stuff that comes out of paint buckets and most of it comes reasonably close to upholding the manufacturer's claims with respect to how much and what sort of protection it will afford.

So write to a manufacturer whose products interest you and ask for one of his booklets on how, when and where to apply the coating. When you get it, give the text a thorough study and follow its guidance for your kind of boat. There are different paints for wooden hulls, metal hulls and fiberglass hulls, and there are some surface coatings that are supposed to work well on all of them.

Most fiberglass boats are delivered with the color impregnated in the hull. They will require little more than a good scrubbing and a little touching up now and then—until the color fades, or you decide on a change—for topsides and deck, that is. The bottom will have to have anti-fouling protection just like any other boat unless you want to grow a hayfield.

If it is not tucked away in a boathouse, or hauled out after every use and trailed home to the family garage, exposure to all sorts of weather, to sun and rain and hail and dampness and marine growths is the normal lot of a boat. To combat these forces—abrupt temperature changes and natural wear and tear—your boat must have the protection afforded by high quality marine surface coatings. Cheap paints and varnishes won't do the job. They may look bright and snappy when first applied, but they simply will not stand up. Poor quality varnish will bubble and darken; low caliber paint will blister and peel. When this happens, you have to clean it all off and start over again. What have you saved?

ESSENTIALS OF GOOD CARE

Assuming that a wooden boat is the object of our attention, here are a few tips on its care:

If paint or varnish is abraded so that bare wood is exposed to the weather, get busy with sandpaper and brush, and patch it.

If you keep your boat in salt water, especially in warm salt water, discourage weeds, barnacles and worms with anti-fouling bottom paint. Occasional rubbing with canvas or scrubbing with a stiff brush will keep down the growth.

If you haul your boat up frequently on sandy, gravelly beaches better have a hard finish for the bottom; perhaps one of the new epoxy base coverings.

If your boat is of plank and frame construction and has been out of the water for some time, the chances are that it will leak when put overboard. That means that the planking has dried, thereby opening the seams between planks. If the drying-out has not been too severe, the planks will swell after the boat has been in the water for a while and the seams will close. If they don't, then you have a job on your hands. Haul the boat out again, clean the leaky seams and force into them a mixture of turpentine and marine glue. The turpentine will evaporate and leave the glue to seal the seams, and it will "give" as the planks dry and swell. There are any number of good prepared elastic seam compounds on the market if you prefer to use them.

When you are going to paint any kind of a boat—wood, aluminum, steel, fiberglass—be sure that it is scrubbed free of dirt, oil and grease. That goes for the outside as well as the interior and the bilges. A good paint job on a wooden hull makes it less likely to soak up oil and grease. Work from the top down when you are painting and do the job on a dry day.

All boats, no matter what their basic material, should be kept clean inside and out. And dry, too. Water comes aboard in the form of rain, spray and the burden of wet bathing suits. It can be removed with pump, bailing can, or sponge. Don't leave water sloshing about under the floor boards. If, between trips, your boat is left on the beach or on a float, turn it upside down to keep the rain out; that is, of course, unless you enjoy bailing and sponging.

Every boatman should have a small but reasonably complete kit for routine maintenance jobs. It should contain a chamois cloth (either genuine or one of the new synthetics which cost a fourth as much as the real skins); varnish spray applicator; small cans of touch-up paint for topsides, deck and bottom; bilge cleaning compounds (for larger boats); seam compound (for planked boats); fiberglass patching and repair kit (for wooden and fiberglass boats); canvas preservative for spray shields, tops and cockpit covers; a can of light oil for blocks and snaphooks.

The chamois can be used to wipe moisture off the fire extinguisher, deck hardware and fittings, to say nothing of sopping up water or dew from seats, rails and varnished surfaces. Varnish takes quite a beating in salt water so all brightwork should be wiped down with fresh water to remove salt deposits after a day's activities. It is a minor chore, but it will save a big job later—using varnish remover and sandpaper on dark, salt-pitted brightwork, and building up new coats of varnish. It takes five coats to do the job thoroughly. Nicks, scratches and scuffs in brightwork can be touched up quickly with the varnish spray applicator.

Gouges in rails and topsides should be filled with plastic wood, marine dough, or one of the polyester or epoxy resin compounds for patching jobs, then painted or varnished.

Promptly and neatly executed touch-ups not only keep your boat looking its best, but prevent water and weather from getting at exposed spots. Checking the condition of the boat's bottom is no problem if it is a trailer transported craft, or one small enough to be beached periodically for examination.

In some waters, particularly those frequented by commercial vessels, pleasure boat waterlines and topsides will acquire soot and oil streaks. These can be removed by the application of a gentle abrasive cleanser, scrubbing brush and elbow grease. If waterline and bottom tend to grow marine gardens, haul the boat out on a float or the beach, scour the fouled parts vigorously with a stiff brush, then touch up any bare places.

If the boat's bottom is merely slimy, a good rubdown with rough canvas will clean it. This is the method employed by keen racing skippers to keep their boat bottoms slick. This kind of a bottom polishing job can be done with the help of a skin diver's snorkel while the boat is overboard. A clean bottom is a fast bottom whether it is on a racing sloop or an outboard runabout.

Dock and anchor lines, lifejackets, cushions and canvas-covered fenders are bound to get wet on small boats; but they do not have to remain so. If your lines are all nylon or dacron, your lifejackets, cushions and fenders covered with plastic-coated fabric, then your troubles are minimized. A few minutes in the sun and they will be dry. Manila rope and canvas need longer drying periods and must not be stowed while damp; that encourages mildew and rot.

When coiling down line to dry, do so loosely so that the maximum of sun and air can get to all parts of it. Coiling it figure-of-eight fashion is one way of doing it. Never "flemish down" line (making tightly coiled, flat mats) when it is wet. It looks pretty, of course, but it stays wet underneath and may mark the deck to say nothing of starting rot in itself.

When lines are dry and ready for stowing they should be coiled—coiled with the lay, or clockwise (with the sun, the old seamen used to say)—and fixed so that the coil won't fall apart

Properly coiled line

and precipitate a snarl. With the coil held in your left hand and the last few feet of line in your right, make two or three turns around the coil, pull them tight, make a half hitch over the top of the coil to lock the turns and then pass the bitter end through the eye of the coil above the turns. Heavy anchor line can be coiled on deck and held in its circular form by lashing it in three or four places with light line.

Having coiled all of the ship's lines, stow them in clean, dry, well ventilated places. This brings up a point: if your boat has a cabin or enclosed cuddy, make certain that it has some means of ventilation—louvres in the hatch door, ports that can be left slightly ajar, or a conventional cowl ventilator. A clean flow of air through enclosed spaces is the enemy of dry rot. Lift up the floorboards in the cabin, too, and let the air circulate through the bilge. If you have wet sails, take them ashore to dry, or spread them loosely about the cabin; don't leave them stuffed soggily into their bags, even if they are made of dacron or some other synthetic fabric.

MOTORBOAT MAINTENANCE

Now a word for those who have outboard motors for their main or auxiliary means of propulsion. The modern outboard is quite a simple, efficient piece of machinery. Take good care of it and it will take good care of you. Neglect its few needs and you'll get the trouble you deserve.

Anyone who can read, who can tell the difference between a sparkplug and a propeller, who can use pliers, wrench and screwdriver, also can keep an outboard engine running. With every new outboard motor comes a manual of operation and upkeep. If you buy a used motor, ask the person from whom you purchased it for the original manual. If he doesn't have it, a note to the manufacturer will bring you one. For that matter, the major oil companies distribute on request somewhat similar but less detailed handbooks on maintenance and lubrication procedures. Keep a motor manual handy for reference and study.

After you have absorbed the more important points made by the engine handbooks, all you will need from then on is a modicum of patience, a kit of simple tools and some common sense.

With few exceptions, American outboard engines are the two-cycle type. They are lubricated by mixing oil with the gasoline before it is drawn into the motor through the carburetor. Oil and fuel must be thoroughly mixed *before* being poured into the tank. The mixing can be done in a clean, airtight can filled to not more than three quarters of its capacity. It doesn't matter which goes into the can first, oil or gasoline, but it does matter that their blending is complete before the mixture is poured through a fine mesh screen into the tank from which the motor will be fed. Beware of sparks, lighted cigarettes, cigars or pipes, and any open fire when the mixing and fueling operation is in progress.

When refilling the gasoline tanks of an outboard boat, do it on the pier or ashore, if possible, so that there will be no fuel spillage on board. If the tanks are more or less permanently fixed in the boat and fuel pump nozzle must be brought aboard be certain that all hatches are closed, stoves are shut down and that no one is smoking. If any spillage occurs, wipe it up carefully. If the motor is electric starting, don't touch the starter if there is any smell of gasoline in bilges or cabin.

Keep sparkplugs clean and properly gapped, keep wiring in

good condition, make certain that there is always plenty of grease in the lower unit, and your troubles will be few. Outboard service stations are numerous along the waterways and in boating communities, but something may go wrong when you are no-where near a professional mechanic. Hence the necessity for carrying extra shear pins, cotter pins, sparkplugs, ignition connections and a few tools—and knowing how and when to use them. An extra propeller is a good idea, too.

There are four things that can put your motor out of working order; that is, there are four *common* causes of failure: ignition, compression, shear pins (on engines that still use them) and fuel. Remember that the engine manual tells the whole story. Here we will go into some of the fundamentals of trouble-shooting. If the engine refuses to start, or quits after running, check the fuel system first by getting answers to these questions:

Is the filler cap vent closed or clogged?
Is the shut-off valve open?
Is there gasoline in the tank? (Boatmen have been known to forget to tend their fuel supplies.)
Are there any obstructions in the fuel line or screen?
Is the filter element on the engine clean?
Is the filler cap on the tank tightly closed and sufficient pressure pumped into it?

If the trouble isn't in the fuel system, next turn to the ignition:

Have the sparkplugs been fouled by surplus oil in the fuel mixture?
Are the plugs corroded, cracked, or chipped?
Do you have the correct gap between plug electrodes?
Are any wires loose or broken?

Now for the fuel itself:

Are gasoline and oil in proper proportion as specified for your engine?
Is there water in the fuel? (It can get there by condensation if a partially full gasoline tank is left overnight with the vent open.)

If the trouble is none of these things, it could be lack of compression:

Is the cylinder head gasket blown out?
Are piston rings clogged with carbon?

Are pistons or cylinder walls worn? (If so, you've got a job for a good mechanic.)

If the motor is running but the prop is not turning, the trouble probably lies with a broken shear pin (in older motors), or in the gear shifting system. These things can happen. Know how to find them and take corrective action. A good seaman can be a reasonably good mechanic, too.

TIPS FROM THE BOS'N

A good way to insure an early Spring launching is to do the routine clean-up jobs and primary painting just before the boat is laid away for the winter.

Air vents in a boat's winter cover will keep the boat from "sweating" and provide essential ventilation. It is a good idea to have such vents in boat covers even if they are left on only a few days at a time. A well made cover is a good investment.

If you have brass deck hardware (cleats, chocks, etc.) a light coating of oil put on them before you leave the boat will make next week-end's cleaning job easier.

CHAPTER 8

The Weather and
What You Can Do About It

·You have, of course, heard times without number the old saw: "Everyone talks about the weather, but no one does anything about it." Not strictly accurate, not in its entirety at any rate.

Fortunately for the boating fraternity, someone *does* do something about the weather besides make it a topic of conversation—the United States Weather Bureau forecasts the weather and warns of storms, and radio stations and newspapers spread the reports.

The boatman can do something about it, too. He can enjoy the good weather, and either avoid or battle the foul by learning something about wind, clouds, barometer, thermometer—individually and collectively.

If there is anyone more conscious of weather than a farmer it is a seaman. The man who steers a boat has at least as keen an interest in the sky as does the man who guides a plow or runs a mowing machine.

The sailor's activities are almost completely governed by weather. The youth who races a slippery little sloop likes to know in advance of a contest whether to bend on full, lightweight sails for gentle breezes, or flat, heavy stuff designed to get the most out of wind that blows with authority. The cruising man's decision on the length and direction of the day's passage, or, indeed, whether to move at all from a snug mooring will be guided—or should be—by the weather. Flexible itineraries often are governed by weather; rigid schedules are upset by it. It isn't enough to know that the sun is shining and the breeze soft when you are preparing to start the day's run; you want to know what it is going to be like at your destination, or what you are likely to run into on the way back. Hence the necessity for reading weather bulletins, studying weather maps, tuning in on radio stations which broadcast full reports for your area, and learning something about local weather signs.

Familiarity with the idiosyncrasies of local weather is just as important to a boating devotee as knowledge of local tides, currents, channels, obstructions and anchorages.

One of the first things to learn about weather—bad weather, that is—is not to fool around with it. Naval aviators have a wonderful admonition for chance-takers: "There are no old, bold pilots." This can be paraphrased for our purposes as: "There are few old, bold boatmen; very few indeed."

If you see thunderheads piling up in the sky, and ominous dark clouds coming your way, stay ashore; don't go looking for trouble. If you're out on the water when these conditions arise, head for the beach or shelter in a hurry. You can always go out again after the squall passes.

Every boatman should know the Weather Bureau's storm signals:

Small craft warning—A red pennant flown at Coast Guard stations, some marinas and yacht clubs to indicate winds up to 38 mph and/or sea conditions dangerous to small boats.

Gale warning—Two red pennants to indicate winds from 39 to 54 mph.

Whole gale warning—A single square red flag with square black center to indicate winds from 55 to 73 mph.

Hurricane warning—Two square red flags with black centers to indicate that winds of 74 mph and above are forecast.

MEETING A SQUALL

If you are out on the water, get hit by a squall and can't get to shelter, keep your wits about you and take the necessary steps for the safety of your boat and her passengers.

This is for motorboats. If it is too deep to anchor and veer a lot of line, have all of your passengers sit in the bottom of the boat to reduce wind resistance and lower the center of gravity, then head the little ship into the wind and move ahead just fast enough to hold her so. If the engine quits and you can't anchor, a bucket dragged astern will keep the boat stern to the wind and slow the rate of drift.

With the motorboat headed into the wind against a squall, the passengers sit in the bottom.

Now for the "rag and stick" sailors, those who have sails and masts to worry about when a squall is imminent. The first item on the agenda is to get sail off. Start with the mainsail. Let it come down on the run, get the boom into the boom crutch, secure the mainsheet and lash the sail securely to the boom. In the meantime you should have cast your jibsheets off the cleats, so that if the squall hits while you are engaged with the mainsail, the jib won't fill and precipitate a capsize.

The idea in getting the main off first is that it is bigger and thus more dangerous from the point of view of keeping the boat right side up. The jib, being much smaller in area, can wait. If you have time to douse it after the main is secured, fine and dandy. If not, the worst that can happen to it if the sheets are free is that it might flog itself to pieces in the blow. Better that than a swamping or capsize.

Once the sails are off, swing the boat stern to wind and run before it. If you are being blown into open water, or onto a dangerous lee shore, drag a bucket astern or stream your heaviest anchor line astern in a bight (loop) to cut down the speed.

If the squall turns out to be not too violent, set the jib and jog around under this small amount of sail until the wind has subsided to the point where it is prudent to set the main again.

There is no point in trying to hammer one's way through stormy going with its high winds, rough water and low visibility. Boating is supposed to be fun and boating under those conditions is anything but fun; it can be downright dangerous, especially for the inexperienced boating hand.

With the sails furled, the sailboat runs before the wind, dragging a bucket astern to reduce speed.

USEFUL CLUES

Old wind ship seamen kept weather signs fresh in their minds by memorizing little jingles that had definite applications to certain atmospheric conditions. Some of them are worth remembering even though they appear to oversimplify meteorological formulae. For instance:

Red sky at morning, sailor take warning.
Red sky at night, the sailor's delight.

And this pair about the wind and glass (seaman's name for barometer):

> A veering[1] wind means weather fair,
> A backing[2] wind, foul weather's near.
>
> When the wind backs and the glass falls,
> Be on guard 'gainst gales and squalls.

Weather forecasting is by no means simply a matter of composing pleasant couplets about sun, clouds and rainbows, but it is something about which every good seaman should know enough to keep out of trouble. Weather almost always tips its hand before playing it and the boatman should be able to recognize the telltale signs.

There are many of them; all are fairly definite behavior patterns. When they are recognized and balanced against certain other factors it is possible to come to a reasonably accurate decision as to just what is in store.

Many newspapers, especially in boating areas, publish daily weather maps which are based on the Daily Surface Weather Map issued by the United States Weather Bureau. Sometimes you can find one on the local post office bulletin board, at a Coast Guard station or airport. The latter two, incidentally, are usually glad to reply to courteous requests for weather information.

The United States Weather Bureau publishes a booklet called *Weather Forecasting*. It is recommended for those who wish to delve into the mysteries of the atmosphere and familiarize themselves with the general conclusions that scientists have drawn from their long experience with the behavior of high and low pressure areas, storm tracks and temperature changes. Study of this booklet will help you to understand what the weather map is trying to tell you, but never minimize the importance of local weather peculiarities.

The most valuable item in the amateur forecaster's weather kit is his knowledge of what is going on along his particular stretch of coastline, or in the country behind his favorite lake. No matter how much of the professional forecaster's knowledge he absorbs from books and charts, no matter how much he knows

[1] Shifting clockwise.   [2] Shifting counterclockwise.

about what the weather is doing halfway across the country, this will be of little value to him if he cannot relate it to what he has learned from a careful, systematic analysis of his own local weather patterns.

One weather-wise sailor used to tell youngsters: "The weather we have with us now only tells what kind of weather we're going to have. The longer the time between signs of change, the longer the altered weather will last; the less warning is given, the shorter the period of the new weather." Sometimes he would say almost the same thing in this rhyme:

> Long threaten, long last;
> Short notice, soon past.

Local weather predictions are not reliable for more than 12 hours because the clues rarely give more warning than that. Weather is always on the move and it moves normally at 25 miles an hour. Since our weather moves in a general west-to-east pattern, what is 100 miles to the westward of us at this moment will be with us within four hours or so.

How about our weather clues, our tips on what to expect? Look at the sky. What kind of clouds do you see? Which way are they moving? What direction is the wind on the water or ground surface? How gently, or how vigorously, is it blowing? Is the air dry, or damp? What does the thermometer say? What is the barometer reading and is it rising or falling?

By themselves these signs mean little, but put them together, weigh them in relation to each other and they tell an interesting story—sometimes a bright and pleasant one that you're glad to hear, sometimes quite the opposite.

There are certain broad rules for barometer and wind observations that should be borne in mind when you are studying weather signs. Here they are:

Wind in the easterly quadrant, barometer falling: foul weather on the way.

Wind shifting to the westward, barometer rising: clearing and fair.

Barometer steady, slowly rising: settled weather.

Barometer steady, slowly falling: unsettled or wet.

Barometer rising rapidly: clear, windy.

Barometer falling rapidly: storm on the way.

Better check these rules, though, against local experience. For instance, on the Pacific Coast, local westerly winds, picking up moisture off the ocean and strengthened in velocity by the area's prevailing westerlies, often bring rain. Conversely, east winds coming off the mountain ranges are more likely to be dry. On the Atlantic Coast, local west winds are usually fair, local easterlies wet and cold. There are local peculiarities along the Gulf of Mexico and in the Great Lakes country, too.

Our friends in the United States Weather Bureau have prepared a detailed wind-barometer chart that is worth keeping in the book in which you record your observations. Here it is for reference:

Wind Direction	*Barometer Reduced to Sea Level*	*Indicated Weather*
SW to NW	30.10 to 30.20, steady	Fair for 1 or 2 days; slight temperature changes
SW to NW	30.10 to 30.20, rapid rise	Fair, followed by rain in two days
SW to NW	30.20 and above, stationary	Continued fair; no decided temperature change
SW to NW	30.20 and above, slow fall	Slow rise in temperature; fair for two days
S to SE	30.10 to 30.20, slow fall	Rain within 24 hours
S to SE	30.10 to 30.20, rapid fall	Winds increasing; rain within 12 to 24 hours
SE to NE	30.10 to 30.20, slow fall	Rain within 12 to 18 hours
SE to NE	30.10 to 30.20, rapid fall	Increasing wind and rain within 12 hours
E to NE	30.10 and above, slow fall	In summer with light winds, rain may not fall for several days. In winter, rain within 12 hours
E to NE	30.10 and above, rapid fall	In summer, rain probable within 12 hours. In winter, rain or snow with increasing winds when wind is in NE.

Wind Direction	Barometer Reduced to Sea Level	Indicated Weather
SE to NE	30.00 or below, slow fall	Rain will continue 1 or 2 days
SE to NE	30.00 or below, rapid fall	Rain with high winds, clearing within 36 hours; followed by cold in winter
S to SW	30.00 or below, slow rise	Clear in few hours, fair for several days
S to E	29.80 or below, rapid fall	Severe storm imminent, followed in 24 hours by clearing (and in winter, colder)
E to N	29.80 or below, rapid fall	Severe NE gale and heavy rain
Going to W	29.80 or below, rapid rise	Winter: heavy snow and cold wave; clearing and colder.

READING THE SKY

You don't have to be a meteorological expert to be a weather-wise boating enthusiast. The colors in the sky itself, the appearance of the sun and the shape and density of clouds are among Nature's tips on what is to come in the way of weather. With practice at reading her signs and learning their meaning you can develop keen weather sense.

Here are some of the things you can learn merely by casting an eye overhead once in a while. Bright blue sky usually means fair weather. A vivid red sky at sunset means fair tomorrow—but the same sky at sunrise means foul weather on the way. If the sky is dull and gray at sunset, the next day's weather is likely to be bad, too; but when the sun comes up in the morning out of a gray horizon there's a good day ahead. Fog early in the morning often indicates a clear day after the sun gets up high enough to burn the mist away.

I think that it was Virgil who wrote:

> Above the rest, the Sun who never lies
> Foretells the change of weather in the skies.

Watch and see how much truth there is in his poetry. A weak, washed-out looking sun is a sign of probable rain. If cirrostratus clouds (more of them later) blot out the sun, look for rain. A diffused and glaring white sun at setting time: expect a storm. A bad night usually follows when the sun sets in dark clouds and the barometer drops. The ball-of-fire sunset (remember, "red at night"): fair and warmer the next day.

CLOUDS

Now about those clouds. Merely fog way up there in the air instead of down on the water or land, they are formed when the air aloft is cooled below the point where dew forms.

Good seamen read clouds like the stars, recognize them instantly and know what they portend. Clouds have many shapes and tell those who will look at them many an interesting story. For instance, high clouds traveling across the sky in the opposite direction from lower clouds mean unsettled weather. As a rule, fleecy, light-textured clouds like cotton balls are a sign of fine weather and moderate breezes, just the sort of thing you want for a day afloat. Small, dark, oily-looking clouds are a sign of rain. If, after a spell of good weather, there is an increase of streaks and patches of white clouds on the horizon, it is likely that there will be a change with wind and rain.

These are generalities, of course, because it is manifestly impossible to tell within the space limitations of this book all the lore of clouds. Large, thick volumes have been written about them, their behavior and significance. Here there is room only for elemental treatment of these sky signs, some gay and lovely, others forbidding and ugly.

Listed below are the ten basic types of clouds, with a brief explanation of what to expect when you see them floating lazily across the inimitable, limitless blue, or hurrying windblown to a rendezvous with a storm.

In the cloud listing, the abbreviation in parentheses after the name is its symbol on government weather maps and in meteorological reports: CI for Cirrus, for example.

There are a number of descriptive couplets about clouds that are worth tucking away in a corner of your memory locker; like this one about cirrus:

> Mackerel scales and mares' tails
> Make tall ships carry short sails.

In other words, a sign of a fresh breeze or more. Then there is this verse about cumulonimbus, the thunderstorm cloud:

> When the clouds appear like rocks and towers,
> The earth's refreshed by frequent showers.

Good seamen, warned by what they see in the sky, what they read on the barometer and what they know about wind direction, prepare for the worst. When they see a thin, brown haze on the sea's horizon they check their position and get ready for fog. If an ominously dirty smudge of cloud line appears on the horizon they know that a squall is imminent; and they know, too, that a squall line sometimes comes ahead of a weather front that may bring heavy wind and rain.

Because they know these things and take the proper steps to meet the situation, any surprises they encounter are likely to be pleasant. Not all storms are violent, but it is the better part of judgment to assume that they will be and move accordingly. In a sense, storms are like rattlesnakes: they warn before they strike.

Be sure that you hear—and recognize—the rattle.

The Cloud Chart
Cirrus (CI)

Detached, delicate, fibrous clouds composed of ice crystals; generally white and silky in appearance. Sometimes in lines, tufts and feather-like plumes. (Mares' tails and what is called "mackerel sky.") If they do not increase, if they drift slowly or appear to be motionless, or dissolve as the sun climbs, fair weather. Otherwise rain and hard weather.

Altocumulus (AC)

A layer of flattened globular masses, the smallest elements of the regularly arranged layer being fairly small and thin. Sometimes shaded, sometimes not. The elements are arranged in groups, in lines or waves, sometimes so close together that their edges join. In small, isolated patches, or if dissipating, they indicate fair weather. If piled into domes, beware of thunderstorm. Rain probable when altocumulus appears with altostratus.

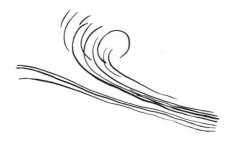

Cirrus

Altocumulus

Cirrocumulus

Cirrostratus

Altostratus

Stratus

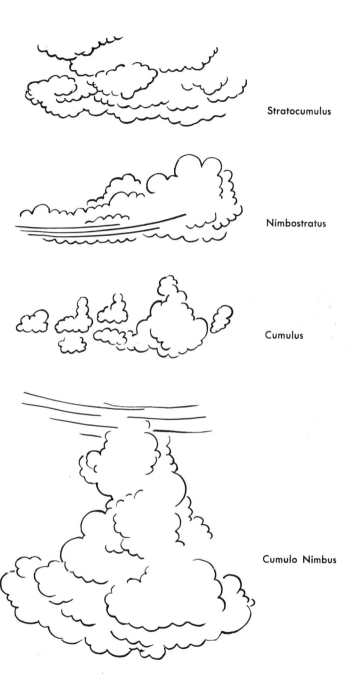

Stratocumulus

Nimbostratus

Cumulus

Cumulo Nimbus

Cirrocumulus (CC)

Sometimes look like ripples in seashore sand; thin layer or patch composed of small white flakes or very small globes arranged in groups or lines indicate approach of weak disturbance, or, if increasing in density, rain in 24 hours.

Cirrostratus (CS)

Thin, whitish veil of fibrous structure which does not blur outlines of sun or moon. Usually causes halos. Sometimes so diffuse that it gives sky a milky look. If these clouds thicken, there will be rain in 6 to 24 hours. If they slip a veil over the whole sky, a warm front or storm is near.

Altostratus (AS)

Striped or fibrous veil, grayish or bluish in color. Resembles thick cirrostratus but does not produce halo. Sun and moon shine through faintly. Sometimes thick and dark enough to hide moon and sun. In this case, differences in thickness result in light and dark patches. Indicates warm front or storm when thickening.

Stratus (ST)

Long, low, uniform cloud layer which looks like fog, but is not resting on ground or water. Expect light, steady rain.

Stratocumulus (SC)

Layer or patch of thin layers, globular masses or rolls. Elements are regularly arranged and smallest are fairly large, soft and gray with darker parts. Often the rolls are so close that their edges join. When they cover the whole sky they have a wavy appearance. When their density increases, look for rain. If they form after showers, weather will clear.

Nimbostratus (NS)

Low, shapeless and rainy layer of dark gray; looks weakly lighted from inside. This is a rain or snow cloud. When it gives precipitation it does so continuously. There is often precipitation which does not reach the ground. In this case, the base of the cloud is scattered and looks wet because of its general trailing precipitation.

Cumulus (CU)

Dense, vertical clouds somewhat like towers. They have a nearly horizontal base and the upper surface is dome-shaped with rounded protuberances. When the sun is behind them, they look dark with a bright edge. With the sun opposite, the surfaces toward the observer are brighter than the edges of the bulges. With the sun on the side, there are strong contrasts of light and shade. If these clouds mass to windward (the direction from which the wind is blowing) they foretell a storm. If they grow in size on a summer day, there will be a thunderstorm. In small, widely separated patches they mean fair weather.

Cumulonimbus (CB)

Heavy masses of cloud growing upward like mountains, the upper parts being fibrous in texture and spreading out into the shape of an anvil. The base resembles nimbostratus with its diffuse trailing streamers which are known as virga. Often the base has below it a layer of very low, ragged clouds. Cumulonimbus is the thunderstorm cloud and generally produces generous showers of rain or snow, and sometimes hail as well.

CHAPTER 9

The Seaman on Wheels

BOATS and wheels go together in this boating age like baked beans and brown bread have for three centuries in New England.

Wheels have released tens of thousands of Americans from the bondage of a land-bound existence, and widened the horizons of tens of thousands more.

Without wheels—those on boat trailers, that is—boating would have been impracticable if not impossible for many who now enjoy it. Without sturdy metal frames and rubber tires on which to transport their craft, others would have had to confine their boating to local waters instead of extending their cruising range as far and wide as time and fancy permitted.

The trailer has done something else, too: it has made back-yard and garage storage of boats commonplace, thereby reducing the cost of boating by eliminating slip and mooring rental fees and commercial care. Moreover, the home-based boat is handy for any cleaning, touch-up or maintenance job, and it is where the owner doesn't have to worry about what is happening to it in bad weather.

On the basis of sales, state license tag issues and other authentic sources of statistics, it has been estimated that there are one and three-quarters million trailers in use in the United States. They range in size from short, light rigs for small craft up to those designed to transport, launch and recover 3,000-pound cruisers.

What have trailers done for those who have teamed them with boats? They have made boating a reality for persons whose homes are a long automobile haul from the nearest pond or stream. They have made it possible for the adventuresome cruising family to explore new lakes, rivers and bays, to go wherever road meets water. For the owner of one of the popular one-design class sailboats, the trailer is the answer to new competitive ventures. He doesn't have to stay at home racing the same adversaries week after week. He can haul his boat onto a trailer, strap it down and head wherever his class is holding a district, regional or national championship or special trophy series.

There are any number of strong, lightweight automobile trailers on the market especially designed and engineered for boats, and virtually all of them are equipped with manual or electric winches to take the hard work out of launching and recovery. More and more waterfront communities are building launching ramps and installing boat lifts for the benefit of the trailer boatman.

THE RIGHT TRAILER FOR YOU

Like everything worthwhile about boating, though, it requires some work and thought to become a master of trailer boating. You must begin with the proper trailer for your particular type of boat. Then you have to learn how to maneuver it behind your car, how to secure the boat safely on the transporter, how to get the boat into and out of the water with the minimum of labor and fuss, and how to keep the trailer and its accessories as shipshape as the boat.

"What kind of a trailer and how big a one do I need?" is a common question. The answer is a series of questions: "What type of boat do you have, how wide and long is it, what does it weigh and how much gear do you plan to carry in it?"

Trailer manufacturers usually describe their products in terms of maximum length and weight they can carry. Obviously, a trailer built to handle efficiently a 12-foot aluminum outboard fishing boat with a 30-pound engine, five gallons of gasoline and a pair of cushions cannot be expected to transport a 20-foot cruiser with twin motors, starting battery, auxiliary fuel supply and a week's supply of water and groceries.

Those who know about such things from experience suggest

that if the total weight of boat, engine and gear is within 100 pounds of the rated capacity of the trailer you are inspecting with a view toward purchase, you should get the next larger model. There is always the chance that you may get a larger boat some day.

Having selected a trailer with the right load capacity you have only done half the job. The trailer has to fit your boat, it has to be long enough to support the hull fore and aft and to ride in proper balance, and its cradle has to be shaped and padded so as to hold and brace the boat in the right places so that it will not "hog" or sag. Be sure that the trailer is so constructed that there is strong support for the transom and that you can travel with the outboard motor clamped in place on the boat.

To make launching and recovery less of a chore and a job which doesn't require a great deal of physical exertion, modern trailers are equipped with tilting booms, elevator type beds, manual and even electrical winches. Unless you are a glutton for labor and don't mind wrestling a boat around in sand and water, make certain that the trailer you select is equipped with up-to-date labor-saving devices. Remember that boating is supposed to be fun.

Your boating equipment dealer should be able to dispense sound advice on what you need in the way of a trailer for your particular boat. After all, his business life depends on the service and consideration he gives to his customers. Keep in mind, too, that the Outboard Boating Club of America (307 North Michigan Ave., Chicago 1, Ill.) certifies the carrying capacity of trailers built by firms associated with OBC and these firms are required to carry spare or replacement parts.

HITCHING AND TOWING

Next on the program is a car hitch, the fitting used for attaching trailer to automobile. A bumper clamp will do if your rig is light and small, but for heavier outfits a hitch which fits directly to the frame of the car is required. Whichever you employ, it is sound safety practice (also the law in some states) to attach a safety chain to the trailer and underbody of the automobile to take over in case something goes wrong with the hitch. Different states have different requirements as to tail and directional lights for trailers, reflectors, safety chains and brakes. Before you go anywhere with your rig be certain that it is equipped to meet the law in the states where it is to be used. The OBC or one of the boating magazines can tell you what you need to know.

There is no special trick or deep mystery about the technique of trailer towing. It merely requires a little more care and a little less speed than you would use normally in handling an unencumbered car on the road. Follow these precautions:

When getting underway, accelerate slowly and shift through all gears to avoid clutch wear.

Drive steadily—about a third slower than the posted maximum on the road you are traveling.

Shift into lower gear going down steep hills.

Anticipate stops, especially if there are no brakes on the trailer.

Allow an extra six inches at the curb when turning corners.

Before passing another vehicle be sure that the road is clear ahead, that you have plenty of room and time in which to carry out the maneuver.

Watch the rear view mirror; if someone is following too closely let him pass. Better that than having him crash into your boat.

Stop at about two-hour intervals to give the outfit a thorough check boat still secured tightly to trailer, boat cover not adrift, hitch all in order, trailer tire inflation all right, lights and directional signals working.

And never forget that you are driving *two* vehicles, not one.

When you first get your trailer and load your boat onto it, take a test drive to familiarize yourself with the rig and the peculiarities of its behavior. Find out in trial runs how much more braking is necessary than with the car alone, how much more distance is needed to bring the combination to a full stop from normal speeds in traffic and on the open road, and how much less acceleration you have. You must know these things if you are to do a safe and efficient job of trailering.

Be sure to put some time in on the backing maneuver and be sure, too, that you do it slowly so that the trailer doesn't jackknife, precipitating embarrassment, confusion or, worse, damage.

When backing a trailer into a parking space, across a beach or down a launching ramp keep this in mind: the stern of the boat (the rear end of the trailer) will swing in the opposite direction to the rear of the automobile. So, for instance, if the trailer jack-knifes slightly to the left in the backing operation, the driver can straighten its course by turning his steering wheel to the right as he backs.

It helps a good deal to have someone behind to signal the driver in the backing maneuver, but a few practice lessons should make one proficent. Backing is just one of those things that have to be learned by doing.

Choice of launching sites is important. There are no problems when the club, municipality or state have provided a concrete or hardtop ramp, or electric lift at your boating site. These,

Evinrude Boating Foundation

Unloading from a trailer into the water

fortunately, are becoming more and more numerous with every passing day. There are still many places, though, where it is necessary to go across a beach to get the boat into the water. In such spots be sure that the ground is solid enough to support car and trailer right to the water's edge and not so soft below that point that the trailer wheels bog down in muck. It is no joy trying to maneuver a trailer in heavy sand, or sticky, oozy mud.

CARE OF THE TRAILER

Maintaining a trailer in good condition is a simple procedure and an inexpensive one, too. It is neglect that eventually costs money. The important things in trailer maintenance are the use of the right kind of lubricant (wheel bearing grease) for the wheels, and keeping the proper air pressure in the tires. Using the wrong grease or not enough in the wheels may result in burned out bearings. An occasional squirt of oil will suffice for the loading winch, rollers and coupling.

If you are a salt water boatman, try to avoid immersing the trailer wheel bearings when launching or picking up the boat. Salt does them no good. Hose the trailer down with fresh water after use and wipe it dry to protect the finish against salt damage. Other jobs are self-evident. For example, where paint is abraded or chipped, touch up the spots with fresh paint; don't allow the cradle padding to wear to the point where the boat is sitting on wood or metal, and be sure that the gripes (the canvas tie-down straps that hold the boat to the trailer) or lashings are not worn, or too old and tired. It is cheaper to buy canvas patches, new rope and straps than it is to repair a boat which has bounced off its trailer because something let go.

If your boat is kept on the trailer through the off season, block the trailer up from the ground or garage floor so that the whole weight of the rig is not resting on the tires. Use the same procedure you would in putting an automobile into dead storage. Be sure, too, that the boat is supported along the full length of the keel and at the widest parts of the hull. You don't want any changes in shape to occur.

The same maintenance rule applies to trailers as applies to boats. Take care of them and they will take care of you; neglect them and they will let you down.

CHAPTER 10

The Compass, Taking Bearings, Reading Charts

IF your boating consists wholly of daylight runs on rivers whose banks are always visible from midstream, or knocking about on familiar narrow lakes whose shores are never out of view, you have no more need of charts and a compass than does the driver of an interstate truck rolling along a throughway he has traveled a hundred times.

Yet no one handling a motorboat, or tending tiller or sheets in a small racing sloop, can pretend to the title of able seaman unless he knows what a compass is, how it functions, how to steer by it and how to use it in conjunction with charts.

Even the person whose activity afloat takes the form of sailing around buoys in confined waters, or tooling an outboard around a two-mile-wide lake needs a sense of direction and the ability to relate his position to those of objects ashore. That's where the compass helps.

To the coast-wise cruising enthusiast, or big lake boatman, the compass is, of course, essential. He cannot go anywhere without one any more than a land surveyor can function without his rod and transit. And charts are his road maps.

The mariner's compass is a relatively simple instrument: basically it is a magnetized bar, or set of bars, affixed to the under side of a circular direction card suspended on a pivot in a bowl of liquid, and always pointing toward magnetic North. Always, that is, unless the magnetic influence of the Pole is thrown out of whack by the presence alongside the compass of a steel wrench, screwdriver, or knife, for instance.

On the inside of the compass bowl are two lubber lines (black vertical lines on the white background of the bowl) diametrically opposed. When the compass is being set in position for use either temporarily or permanently, these lines must be parallel with the fore and aft line of the ship—lined up with the keel, in other words. Since the compass bowl turns as the boat turns, but the card doesn't (boat and bowl turn under it), the forward lubber line always designates on the compass card the direction in which the bow is heading.

The edges of compass cards are divided into degrees (360 of them), into points (32 cardinal points in the sailor's language), or—as is usually the case with modern instruments—into degrees on the outer edge and the points just inside of them on a smaller, concentric circle.

Each of the 32 points is equivalent to $11\frac{1}{4}$ degrees. Sailing vessels used to be steered to courses like "Northeast by East," but nowadays, particularly on cruises and distance races, chances are that the navigator uses the numerical equivalent of five points off North, or 56 degrees. (He'll skip that quarter of a degree—no one can steer that accurately anyhow.)

Even if degrees are used for steering courses, compass points, or directions, are still needed by seamen. Except for aviation pilots, I never heard anyone say that the wind was from "two two five degrees" when it was southwest. And sailors still say that such-and-such a place is northeast of somewhere else. Hence the necessity for learning to "box" the compass and to read its triangles and diamonds as well as the numbers around the card edge.

Now let us take a good look at the compass and see whether we can figure out a relatively easy way of determining what those SW's, NNE's, diamonds and triangles mean.

Everyone, it is assumed, knows the four cardinal points. They are, of course, North (0 degrees on the outer edge); South (180 degrees); East (90) and West (270). In between them are four intercardinal points, also designated by large black triangles. They are, going clockwise, Northeast (45 degrees), Southeast (135), Southwest (225) and Northwest (315).

The next major divisions, midway between cardinal and inter-cardinal points and indicated by large diamonds might be called, for want of a better name, inter-intercardinal points. There are eight of them and their names are compounded from their nearest cardinal points and nearest intercardinal points. For example, North Northeast is named for its nearest cardinal, North, and its nearest intercardinal, Northeast. Then on the other side of North-east there is East Northeast, its nearest cardinal point being East and its nearest intercardinal Northeast. And so on around.

So now we have accounted for sixteen points—four cardinal, four intercardinal and eight inter-intercardinal. We have sixteen left. They are the second-sized triangles halfway between each cardinal and its nearest inter-intercardinal point and halfway between each intercardinal point and its flanking inter-intercardinals. Each of these little points is named for the nearest cardinal point and always has the word "by" in the middle of its compound name; North by East is the first point to the right of

Compass Rose

North, and North by West is the first point to the left of North. Following our system, moving clockwise, the next of these little points after North by East is Northeast by North, Northeast by East, East by North, East by South, etc. Now we are ready to "box" the compass, that is to reel off each of the 32 points starting with North and going around clockwise. In between each point there are four quarter points, but although observed in fine steering and laying out courses, they are not taken into account when boxing the compass.

1.	North	N
2.	North by East	N by E (often written N x E)
3.	North Northeast	NNE
4.	Northeast by North	NE by N (or NE x N)
5.	Northeast	NE
6.	Northeast by East	NE by E (NE x E)
7.	East Northeast	ENE
8.	East by North	E by N (E x N)
9.	East	E
10.	East by South	E by S (E x S)
11.	East Southeast	ESE
12.	Southeast by East	SE by E (SE x E)
13.	Southeast	SE
14.	Southeast by South	SE by S (SE x S)
15.	South Southeast	SSE
16.	South by East	S by E (S x E)
17.	South	S
18.	South by West	S by W (S x W)
19.	South Southwest	SSW
20.	Southwest by South	SW by S (SW x S)
21.	Southwest	SW
22.	Southwest by West	SW by W (SW x W)
23.	West Southwest	WSW
24.	West by South	W by S (W x S)
25.	West	W
26.	West by North	W by N (W x N)
27.	West Northwest	WNW
28.	Northwest by West	NW by W (NW x W)
29.	Northwest	NW
30.	Northwest by North	NW by N (NW x N)
31.	North Northwest	NNW
32.	North by West	N by W (N x W)

The compass has two purposes in life: it indicates the course being steered, and is used to measure angles and to take the bearings necessary for a "fix" to determine position. The compass has two weaknesses: it always points to magnetic North, which is some distance from true North, and it is susceptible to errors induced by magnetic materials nearby.

So when using a compass, the mariner has two factors to bear in mind: variation, the number of degrees of variance between magnetic and true North (the amount differs according to geographical location—zero near Florida and the Bahamas, for instance, and 12 degrees west off New York), and deviation, which is an error in the compass caused by something in the boat (nearby ferrous metal—centerboard, tools, etc.—or electrical devices). Deviation differs on different headings and in different boats; no two are alike.

Variation in any locality is always indicated on the chart for that area. All charts carry on their faces what are known as compass roses. These are two concentric circles, the outer of which, marked in degrees, indicates true directions, and the inner, marked in both degrees and points like a compass, which shows magnetic directions. Then, right in the middle of the rose, will be printed something like this: "Var 12°1′ W 1958; Annual Increase 2′."

This variation must be taken into account when courses or bearings are translated from true magnetic or vice versa. So also must deviation be figured into the course to be steered unless it has been eliminated by an adjustment of the compass to correct it. But this is an area for more advanced yachtsmen. The seaman needs to know that variation and deviation exist and are worth some of his study time, but for most practical small boat purposes he can get along with compass and the inner circle on the chart's compass rose. After all, he is primarily interested in determining where he is and how he is going to get from there to where he wants to go in poor visibility.

FINDING LOCATION AND USE OF CHART

A simple method for determining your location on the water by means of chart and compass and such simple tools as parallel rules, pencil and dividers is by taking bearings on objects ashore, or aids to navigation that are easy to see.

This is the procedure for getting cross bearings and a "fix." Sight over the compass (along an edge of parallel rules or a piece of cardboard, if you like) at, let us say, a water tank whose location is plotted on the charts. When you have lined up the tip of your ruler or straight edge with the tank, note the point or degree on the compass where your sighting instrument crosses the edge of the card.

Now take the parallel rules, lay them across and through the exact center of the nearest compass rose on your chart until they line up with the figure you picked off the compass. Let's call it 90 degrees, or NE, for the purposes of this example. Now "walk" the parallel rules across the chart to the tank on which you sighted. With a sharp pencil, draw a line a few inches long from the tank out along the edge of the rule. That's one bearing.

We need another, so follow the same sighting, "walking" and line-drawing procedure with another object—a lighthouse, or radio tower, for instance—so located that the angle from the first object will be not less than 30 degrees and preferably nearer 90. Where the line from the second bearing crosses the first is your "fix" or position.

Having determined where you are, it is an easy matter to lay off your course to the next buoy or place you want to reach. Lay the parallel rules down on the chart, connecting your position with that of, say, a beacon you must pass. Draw a line between them and then "walk" the rules to the nearest compass rose, split that little cross in the middle and read the direction lined up by your ruler. That is your course. Write it on the line you just drew and with it the reciprocal, or opposite, course. You may come that way again.

In small boat piloting, it is the general practice to use the inner compass circle on the chart rose for courses and bearings because it corresponds to the boat's compass and so makes it unnecessary to fuss around with additions or subtractions for westerly and easterly variation between true and magnetic. The simpler you keep small boat navigation, the less chance there is for error.

The charts made by the United States Coast and Geodetic Survey and the Lake Survey are rather wonderful pieces of work in their accuracy and detail. But they take careful reading and a working knowledge of their symbols which indicate rocks, shoals, wrecks, deep water, buoys, lighthouses and everything else needed to guide the seaman. All of these are explained on the chart itself.

Charts have been called the road maps of the sea and no seaman worthy of the name should embark on even a day's cruise without a large scale detail chart of the area of operation. Charts are easy enough to obtain and the cost is slight.

The United States Coast and Geodetic Survey, Washington 25, D.C., makes charts for coastal waters and adjoining navigable rivers, and also compiles current tables and draws tidal current charts. These publications and Light Lists (location and characteristics of various lighted aids to navigation) may be obtained from the Superintendent of Documents, Washington 25, D.C., or from field offices and sales agencies in major ports.

For charts of major inland rivers the sources are the numerous offices of the Corps of Engineers, United States Army. For charts of the Great Lakes, Lake Champlain, and New York States canals, try the United States Lake Survey, 630 Federal Building, Detroit 26, Michigan.

Sailor Language

Glossary of Boating Terms

To THE uninitiated, the language of the seaman is mysterious, confusing and wholly unrelated to shore-going English. To those familiar with it, the language is precise and explicit; rarely does a word have more than one meaning.

Some words, some expressions, have been used at sea for centuries, but the nautical tongue is not static, no more so than any other language. With the passing of the square-riggers many words have passed, too; there is no longer any use for them. With the coming of steam and motor, new words found their way into the sailor's lexicon.

What follows is an abridged dictionary for the boatman, one which contains enough salty words and their meanings to help him understand the average boat yard and boat club conversation, and to know what authors of marine literature and nautical publications are trying to tell him.

ABAFT. Toward the stern; behind.

ABEAM. Used in reference to the position of an object; at right angles to the fore-and-aft (center) line of the boat. (For example, another boat, a buoy, or lighthouse is abeam when it is abreast of your boat.)

ABOARD. On or in the boat.

ADRIFT. Not made fast; lying around loose.

AFT. At or near the stern, or rear end, of the boat.

AMIDSHIPS. Halfway between bow and stern; in the middle.

ANCHORAGE. A sheltered area where boats can anchor in reasonable safety and not interfere with harbor traffic.

ASTERN. Behind the boat; backwards. (An object is astern when it is behind the boat. A boat is going astern when it is moving backwards.)

AWEIGH. Said of an anchor when it is clear of the bottom.

BACKSTAY. Wire brace led aft to support the mast.

BARNACLE. A form of marine life which grows on boat bottoms in salt water. A crop of barnacles will markedly reduce a boat's speed.

BEAM. Greatest width of boat. (A boat is said to have 9-foot beam when it measures 9 feet at its widest part.)

BEAM SEA. A sea running at right angles to the boat's course; a sea that is abeam, in other words.

BEAR AWAY (or Off). Sail away from the wind, rather than hold up to it.

BELAY. A command to stop. A line is belayed when it is made fast.

BELAYING PIN. A wooden or metal pin fitted into a rail for the securing of sheets and halyards.

BELOW. In the cabin, or under the deck.

BEND. What you do with sails when you fit them onto their spars, or what you do with lines. You don't *tie* two lines together, or *tie* them to things; you *bend* them together, and you *bend* a line on an anchor, for instance.

BIGHT. Any part of a rope except the end; usually refers to a loop in the rope.

BILGE. Curved or angular part of the hull where bottom and sides meet; also the space under the cabin floor or the cockpit floorboards.

BINNACLE. Protective casing for the compass.

BITTER END. The last part of a rope, or the last links in an anchor chain.

BOLLARD. A short, heavy post on pier or wharf for docking lines.

BOOM. Pole or spar to which the foot (lower edge) of a sail is bent—attached, that is.

BOOM CRUTCH. A notched, upright board or metal structure into which the boom fits when sail are furled.

BOOT TOP. A narrow stripe of paint at the waterline accenting the division of topsides and bottom.

Bow. Forward, or front end of boat.

Bow Chocks. Metal fittings on deck at the bow through which anchor and dock lines are led.

Break Out. To unfurl (as a flag, or sail); to remove from its storage space (a can of beans from the bilge, for instance).

Brightwork. Varnished surfaces; polished brass or chrome fittings.

Bunk. A sailor's delight; his bed.

Bulkhead. Partition, or wall between compartments.

Buoy. A floating marker usually anchored to the bottom. There are mooring buoys (to mark moorings), net buoys (on fishermen's nets), buoys on lobster pots, racing buoys and, of course, the markers that the government puts in place to keep sailors away from hazards.

Cable Length. 100 fathoms, or 600 feet.

Carry. The forward momentum of a boat after its engine has been stopped, or (in the case of a sailboat) has come up into the wind.

Caulk. To make seams watertight by filling them with cotton, oakum, or caulking compound.

Ceiling. A lining of thin planking on the inside of ribs, or frames, of a boat.

Centerboard. A movable plate of wood or metal that can be raised or lowered through the keel of the boat. In the down position, the centerboard increases the boat's draft, stability and lateral resistance.

Chart. Marine version of road map, showing aids to navigation, shoals, water depths, dangers, etc.

Chafing Gear. A wrapping of canvas or rope around spars, rigging, or lines to prevent chafe.

Cleat. A horned fitting of wood or metal to which lines are belayed (made fast).

Clew. The lower after corner of a sail.

Closehauled. Sailing close to the wind.

Coaming. Sides of cockpit above the deck line to keep water out.

Cockpit. Open part, or well, of boat where passengers sit and the helmsman usually does his work.

Cuddy. Small partitioned space under the foredeck for storage.

CRINGLE. A ring sewn into the sail so that a line can be passed through it. (Clew cringle, tack cringle, reefing cringle, etc.)

DAVIT. A curved metal spar projecting over the side or stern for lifting and lowering small boats; sometimes used forward to handle anchors on large craft.

DEADLIGHT. A heavy circular glass lens set flush and permanently into deck or bulkhead to admit light.

DITTY BAG. A small bag for carrying or stowing small articles.

DITTY BOX. Hinged lid box for the same purpose.

DRAFT. Depth of hull from water line to lowest point of keel.

DRY ROT. Something you shouldn't have in a boat; decay in wood caused by fungus infection usually stemming from poor ventilation.

EMBARK. Go on board.

EASE. Slacken.

FAKING DOWN. A method of coiling rope so that each fake (flat coil) overlaps the preceding one and is free for running out rapidly.

FATHOM. A measure: 6 feet.

FLOTSAM. Floating wreckage, trees, brush, driftwood and the like.

FLOORS. Short timbers bolted across the keel and to which frames are fastened for added structural strength.

FLUKE. The flattened end of an anchor arm.

FORE AND AFT. In a line with the keel.

FOUL. Not clear; jammed.

FRAME. A boat's rib.

FREEBOARD. The distance from waterline to main deck or rail.

GALLEY. Boat's kitchen.

GEAR. General name for ropes, blocks, tackle and equipment.

GROUND TACKLE. The anchor and anchoring gear.

GUNWALE. Pronounced "gun'l"; upper edge of a boat's side or rail.

HATCH. Opening through deck or cabin to area below.

HALYARD. A line used for hoisting sail.

HEAD. A boat's toilet.

HEAVE. To throw (as a line ashore); the rise and fall of a vessel in a seaway.

HEAVE IN. To pull (as on an anchor line).

HEAVING LINE. A light line, or messenger, attached to a heavier line and thrown to a pier or another vessel.

HEEL. A boat heels when it inclines to one side or the other.

HELM. The device with which one steers (tiller, wheel).

HELMSMAN. The one who steers.

HULL. The main body or shell of the boat. Does not include deckhouses, flying bridges and the like; they're superstructure.

IRISH PENNANT. An untidy loose end of rope.

JETSAM. Things which sink when thrown overboard (they don't float like flotsam).

JIB. A triangular sail set forward of the mast.

JIBSHEET. The line by which the trim of the jib is controlled.

JIBE. Bringing a sailboat from one tack to another by swinging her stern (not bow) through the wind to bring the breeze from one quarter to the other.

JURY RIG. A makeshift.

KEEL. The boat's backbone; the main timber extending from stem to sternpost.

KING SPOKE. The upper spoke of a steering wheel when the rudder is amidships, usually marked in some fashion.

KNOT. A measure of speed on the water—a nautical mile (distance) per hour.

KNOCK OFF. To stop doing something, particularly work; when a helmsman of a sailboat is ordered to "knock her off," he steers a course further from the wind.

LANDFALL. The first sighting of land when coming in from sea.

LANDLUBBER. What you aren't when you go to sea.

LANYARD. A rope made fast to an article, i.e., knife lanyard, bucket lanyard.

LAZARETTE. A small space below decks in the after part of some vessels, usually used for storage of gear.

LEEWARD. Pronounced for no good reason "loo'ard." The direction away from the wind.

LEEWAY. Drift to leeward, or in the direction toward which the wind is blowing.

LIMBER HOLES. Holes in floor timbers to allow bilgewater to drain into the lowest part of the hull.

LOCKERS. Closets.

LOG.   Record book of vessel's activities; an instrument for measuring distance sailed or steamed.

LUFF.   The forward or entering edge of a sail. To "luff up" is to sail directly into the wind to miss an object, or to reduce the boat's speed.

MAINSAIL.   The sail set on and abaft the mainmast; the boat's main or principal sail.

MAINSHEET.   The line by which the trim of the mainsail is controlled.

MIZZENMAST.   The after and shorter of two masts on yawls and ketches.

OUTBOARD.   Toward the sides of a vessel, or outside of it.

OUTHAUL.   A device and/or line used to haul out the clew, or after corner, of a sail along a boom.

OVERALL (length).   The extreme fore-and-aft measurement of a boat on deck.

OVERHANG.   The projection of the bow and stern beyond the waterline.

PAINTER.   Shorter piece of line secured in the bow of a dinghy for towing it or making it fast.

PAY OUT.   Slack away on a line made fast on board.

PIPE DOWN.   An order to be quiet.

PORT.   Left. (A boat's port side is that on the left looking forward.)

QUARTER.   That part of a craft lying within 45 degrees from the stern; starboard or port quarter depending on whether reference is to right or left corner.

RAIL.   Boat's side above deck line.

RIP (tide).   Short, steep waves kicked up by strong tidal currents.

SHEER.   The upward curve or sweeps of a vessel's deck line.

STAFF.   Upright pole to which flag or light is affixed.

STARBOARD.   Right. (Starboard side is the right side looking forward.)

STEM.   More or less vertical timber at bow; boat's entering edge.

STERN.   After, or back, end of boat.

SWAB.   Sea-going name for mop. (You swab down, not mop up.)

THWART.   A transverse seat in a boat.

THWARTSHIPS. At right angles to the fore-and-aft line.

TILLER. A length of wood or metal fitted into the rudder head, or outboard motor, by which the boat is steered.

TOPSIDES. Sides of hull above waterline.

TRANSOM. The board or boards forming the after end of a boat whose stern is not pointed, or canoe-style; in outboard boats it is that part of the boat which the engine is suspended.

TRICK. A period of duty at the helm.

TURNBUCKLE. A metal appliance consisting of a thread and screw capable of being tightened or slacked, and used in setting up stays on a sailboat's mast. Sometimes called a rigging, or bottle screw.

TRIM. The way in which a boat floats. If she leans to one side or the other, she is said to be "listing" to port or starboard as the case may be. If she is too heavily loaded forward and the bow is depressed, she is "trimmed by the head." If she is weighed down aft, she is "trimmed by the stern." When she is balanced on her lines she is "on an even keel."

UNDERWAY. A boat is underway when she is moving through the water. (Technically she is underway when her dock lines are cast off, her anchor is aweigh, or she is not aground.) She makes headway going forward, sternway when going backward, and leeway when being set sideways by the wind.

UNSHIP. To take apart or remove from its place.

VEER. To slack off and allow to run out (like veering more anchor line); a change in wind direction.

WAY ON. Movement of a boat through the water.

WEATHER SIDE. The windward side, the side toward the wind.

WINDWARD. The direction from which the wind is blowing.

YAW. A vessel "yaws" when it swings widely from one side of the course to the other, usually when running before heavy quartering seas.

Index